P9-AFZ-275

Coming to Life

Coming to Life

Leston Havens

Harvard University Press

Cambridge, Massachusetts, and London, England   1993

Copyright © 1993 by Leston Havens

All rights reserved

Printed in the United States of America

10 9 8 7 6 5 4 3 2 1

This book is printed on acid-free paper, and its binding
materials have been chosen for strength and durability.

Library of Congress Cataloging in Publication Data

Havens, Leston L.

   Coming to life / Leston Havens.

      p.   cm.

   ISBN 0–674–14432–5

   1. Self.   2. Psychotherapy.   3. Psychotherapist
and patient.   4. Identity (Psychology)   5. Self-
actualization.   I. Title.

RC489.S43H38   1993

616.89' 14—dc20   92–23563

CIP

Designed by Gwen Frankfeldt

To Susan Miller-Havens, wife and friend,
these pages are gratefully inscribed,
for her gift of the real

Contents

It is when we try to grapple with another man's intimate need that we perceive how incomprehensible, wavering, and misty are the beings that share with us the sight of the stars and the warmth of the sun.

—Joseph Conrad, LORD JIM

~Introduction

The work of healing begins in a safe place, which then exposes what is false and what is real. It is no easy task to exchange one for the other.

I pass a stranger on the street; a flash of color, the toss of hair, perhaps a gesture or the almost lurching amble of the walk stirs me. I imagine a seemingly whole person, even part of a lifetime between us. This moment has the force of a fetish in its exchange of part for whole, a rounding out as well as an imaginative filling in. Marriage, too, as often as not begins with this falling in love. Then gradually a real person appears whom we may be able to love. What constancy it takes, what grasp of the real, to transform the first wild hopes.

Marcel Proust saw a comparable process at the center of the novelist's power: "none of the feelings aroused in us by a real person's joy or misfortune can be produced except through the intermediary of an image of that joy or misfortune. The first novelist's ingenuity lay in understanding that, as the image is the one essential element in the structure of our emotions, to simplify it by suppressing the real person would be a decided improvement. A real person, however deeply we may sympathize with him, is in large part perceived through our senses; that is, he remains opaque, offers a dead weight that our imagination cannot lift" (*Du côté de chez Swann,* NRF edition, 1:81–82).

We are all concerned with the images we display for the interpretation of others. Clinically we do much the same thing, turning those words around: the interpretations of others we display professionally create an image between us as well. Today narcissism is an idea that therapists often bring to patients. But these pointings, to someone's walk, to a character in fiction, to narcissism, are only pointings. They don't tell us what else may be present or the relation of that fuller psychological life to what is pointed out. These last wait upon our penetrating the opaque, a full coming to life.

By *coming to life* I mean something that has many names: the emergence of a real person, self-possession, psychological being, selfhood, soul. Bear with me here, as I try to wrest these terms from their subjective, mystical, artistic settings. The earliest physiologists, struggling to understand the breath and blood that animate the body, were just as pitiable in their talk of spirits and humors giving life to flesh. The first and last sign of life was once thought to be breath. The soul was believed to be in the diaphragm, so that breath and soul arose together. Now life is more likely to be detected electrically, perhaps in the brain, and there has been until recently little scientific talk of soul. But the great contentions around abortion and euthanasia push forward such ideas as viable human being, personhood, and the different meanings of death, as do patients who seem mechanical or absent. It is, then, ever more pressing to define psychological life.

The neurologist Oliver Sacks has made it a central topic: brain and body, in growing contact with nature and society, develop a unique identity or selfhood that at once links them to and comprises a meaningful construction of the world. Experience with brain-damaged patients reveals that restoration of this identity makes possible extraordinary gains in performance. Students of the psychoses, and of everyday life, know as many or more examples.

This book approaches the definition of selfhood from the psychological side, from the study of patients in a psychotherapy informed by literature and art as well as science. Just as neurology describes levels of brain integration, so we must shape psychological perception to discern states leading up to a full psychological life. It is not enough to define it. We must recognize and nourish it. Medicine has many tests of physical life and health; it seldom speaks as psychologists and psychiatrists speak, calling patients depressive, psychotic, borderline, as if they were all one or the other. The medical patient has a tumor in the bladder wall; the great bulk of tissues are well. Listen to a thousand psychiatric-hospital case conferences for one word of health. We may not be guilty, but we are all psychologically sick until proved very innocent indeed. Everything that follows is intended to show how psychological health is recognized and how it emerges and can develop.

We seldom can be sure whether the difficulty in finding the real person rises from our imaginative failure or from the others' inability to appear. Sometimes they are only hiding, waiting for us, to see if the real person in us can be found and trusted. We may go to the end of a long treatment and not know if the person who emerged grew in that period or was there all along, only waiting for a clear sign of our reality and safety. Many times one or both seem possessed, the therapists by fixed ideas narrowing the necessary openness to psychological being, the patients by their images of themselves or by the powers of people who own them. If health is to move from possession to self-possession, from image to the real person suppressed, means must be found to compensate for the loss of images, however incomplete. Lucky couples go from being in love to love. What compensates them?

Listen to therapists talking about their patients, especially patients they have known a long time. Again and again, words like brilliant and creative are used. You would think we lived in a community of geniuses. Granted their paying plays a part, and their willingness to come at all, and the significant rewards of being, like our children, ours. But I believe that a large part of this liking, so like a loving, arises from the nature of the work. Two fundamental needs are being met: the need to be ourselves, to express ourselves, and the need to be with others. And this is true of both parties, therapists expressing their work selves. The range of jealousies, ambitions, thwarted hopes, rage, sadness, and joys allies this company of two with human nature at large, makes us one with the delights and despair of the centuries. In the real expression of feeling, we are moved in precisely the way we are moved by great poetry and drama. This is why patients seem so creative. Something is created between us. I am saying that the surrender of labels and images, at least their partial surrender, comes about happily on this common human ground. The lucky couples have the same experience.

I don't mean that patients or loved ones are accepted in a blind attachment. What you accept is what you accept about yourself, the parts of human nature. It requires an element of vigilance and fear, notably of the human capacity for destructiveness. Indeed, what is moving about our encounter with one another is this very element of suffering and danger which, appearing in the patient's life and suffered through with the therapist, moves us and the patient through a danger, not necessarily to safety but to some point beyond what had been. Marriage has many such moments, which have the poignancy of being moments when we might move apart instead of together.

The success of all our relationships depends on the attitude we take toward what we discover, no less what we discover about ourselves. Can we, the word is, understand? Psychotherapy gains its immense power from being able to model that understanding, which has the power to remodel patients' attitudes toward themselves. This is no shallow forgiveness or bland acceptance. Reaching an understanding of one's humanity is no carte blanche for action or sunny accounts of ourselves. It includes the most profound repugnance, the most powerful restrictions on behavior; yet its attitude remains understanding. We end saying of ourselves: I will never forgive myself for that; it is still part of me. I suspect the chief source of our unwillingness to repeat mistakes is this awareness of the deep possibility of their occurrence.

That such an understanding is necessary to relationships springs from the random nature of their occurrence. Therapists do not select their patients from any vast knowing of them; mostly they answer the bell. Marriage, even marriage after the extensive "living together" so common today, is still a shot in the dark. Of course this is partly because of romance and the lure of the erotic or the playing out of roles. But the deepest reason is chance. Bob met Mary because he missed his train and took the bus. She was twenty-nine and desperate; his younger brother had just married. The wildest gambler at Las Vegas never took such chances. And this is even more keenly true in our relationships with ourselves. You didn't pick your body;

you didn't pick your mind, and certainly not your parents. We are about as much responsible for ourselves early in life as we are for outer space. The full and lucky souls emerge. Abraham Lincoln remarked that no one was responsible for his face until he was forty. Hence the need to be able to reach an understanding.

It is no accident that we "practice," as musicians do, knowing that this work of movement depends on our ability to resonate to the wide range of human concerns. The word *practice* also suggests that we never get it right, that we had better try again tomorrow. This applies as much or more to the present efforts of reconstruction. I hope I have made my hypotheses clear enough to alert the reader to the images and theories that vivify and distort these efforts to understand. In addition the cases are disguised, by details making them unrecognizable to many. But in another sense the cases are revealed, because the details chosen are meant to state an emotional truth, so that the patients recognize themselves. I can only work from nature, as some painters say, from memories of the person held before my mind. I want those expressions to act on me. Otherwise I perceive what I expect, since the mind's first tendency is to capture the person in familiar images and concepts. Only when we return to nature from a fresh perspective do we begin to reach what has been suppressed. The result can never be complete; life must be caught as it emerges. Nor is the result accurate in any final sense, since we use our inventiveness in the service of sensations. The observer must be plastic and compliant as well as free and independent. Hence the difficulty of the work.

Imagery

1 ⁓ The Eye of the Beholder

She was tall, thin, with a great mane of chestnut hair and hands that began to speak before she said a word. They were strong hands, long-fingered and graceful, and they pointed, determined space, as if the world were a malleable substance she could make into what she wanted. Later I came to know that she was truly beautiful, that her beauty was not in clothes or makeup. But what first vivified the relationship for me was the image I formed.

Often we experience at the first instant of meeting an impression that never recurs or appears only much later. I remember once being startled at the beginning of a teaching film introduced by a colleague. Ordinarily he was all decision and self-possession. At the start of his brief appearance, it was as if he were in drag: he cavorted in a seductive passivity that came and went in a moment. My patient's brief determination was as settling as his caricatured femininity was unsettling.

As a boy I saw the beautiful actress Hedy Lamarr across the street in a shimmering evening light. She was both real and unreal. She moved, but it is the stillness I remember, the perfect image. When she moved, she moved away, and my mind throws up the image of another actress, Irene Dunne, who looked uncannily like a memory I have of my mother. I believe the bittersweet, melancholy glamor of all three images gains its vividness from that same mother and me, close and moved apart. There is something else here too: only a few are equipped to play such parts. One photographer of Marilyn Monroe wrote that he didn't need to tell her where to stand or how to pose or move. She understood his imaginative promptings before he did. No wonder so many loved her. She could literally bring our imaginations to life, be what we wanted—which may have cost her life.

Later the patient taught me that she did not support the image out of pride; it seldom felt like her. Aesthetically it pleased her; there were also moments when she loved its defiance and superiority to a world otherwise indifferent. But the image was what she thought she ought to be, her ideal. It felt terrible to have an ideal that seemed only an act.

I want to realize what lies behind these first impressions: to re-create the real if either she or I had lost it in attention to the image. We see from the start how hard it is to know whether the failure is in me, in her, or in both of us. Was I captivated by my image of her, or was she hidden from herself in attention to beauty itself? The clinical situation dictates that I cannot contemplate the problem from afar. It is here on top of me right now, so I must act.

I didn't know what to do. I'm sure I enjoyed looking at her, which was at least honest. Clinical work has these unexpected pleasures, as when an ordinary citizen, without fame, glamor, or great money, finds himself face to face with the image of a goddess or a queen. The first time it happened to me I was an intern, white-clad and rumpled, doing my rounds on the private service of a New York hospital. I opened the door, entered a large room, then saw lying in bed against its enormous white pillow a famous beauty of the day. Typically the nurses had not warned me, enjoying the initiation rites of a young intern. Something still more unsettling followed. Right beside her, standing tall, was her equally famous husband. It may all have been an oedipal dream, but I thought he scowled at me, I who was about to disrobe and examine his wife. I fled. But I didn't want to flee from the lady with the chestnut hair.

I could wait, for something to occur to me. I didn't want to have an official or artificial talk, I didn't want to meet the image before me with a separate image of my own. I would have been grateful if a window had opened and a fresh breeze blew in. Then we could have something real and pleasant to talk about, something that was happening to both of us here and now. In a novel by Kingsley Amis, the beautiful lady offers the ugly-duckling hero a cup of coffee they will both drink from. Something like that.

But I couldn't wait too long. Too long a silence would itself have become my intervention, with all its power to unsettle, invite accusations and self-accusations, make either or both of us feel tongue-tied, like adolescents on a first date. And the longer the silence, the more pressure to say something suave, again an image or role. In situations like this, I often find myself thinking, the weather, the weather. If it would not come in by itself, through the window, I could bring it in.

"Has it stopped raining?" I asked. That is one of the advantages of practicing in Boston—always plenty of weather. There are also advantages to discussing it. My remark proved I could talk, and it gave her a question I knew she could answer. It situated us together in a common fate. In a real sense, like the coffee cup, it brought us together. There was also a subtler advantage. Weather is the great Rorschach card, the great vague stimulus on which we all, every day, project our wishes and furies. I put it out in front of us. She might begin to speak freely.

She did not. Instead she revealed the work we had to do. She attended on me. My question immediately set in motion an elaborate, thorough apparatus of concern. If I was worried about rain, some project of my own might be in danger. How could she help? To directly inquire might seem intrusive, so the bulk of her concern must be frustrated, sat on, to her discomfort and sense of guilt. That's how far I was from setting her free.

The extent of this discomfort and guilt I only learned later; all I caught now was a concerned look. But she had allowed me to speculate on the power her combination of beauty and concern could exercise over the men she knew. Certainly it is a combination much advertised. It is the pose women take in advertisements meant to stimulate the purchase of cars, cigarettes, almost everything. The man or the car is there, often both, and the woman looks up worshipfully, concerned, and as beautiful as the imagemakers can design. The woman hangs off the man, like an ornament or accessory. The advertisers know what men want—beauty at their service, Marilyn Monroe.

The largest single support psychotherapy has gained in the decades of my observation has been the women's movement, more, I believe, than the help provided by medications or the broadening out of dynamic thought in existential and interpersonal ways. The women's movement has provided support for recognizing women's servitude and sometimes for organizing their release. Servitude has been no great secret, but the presence of a movement, the speaking out, has certified the situation, given it public support, so the perception is easier to reach and hold. I have been astonished by the frequency with which symptoms, say depression and anxiety, fade simply with the acknowledgment of impossible domestic situations, even before the situations themselves are corrected. Psychological complaints reflect such limitations of human existence, failures to move beyond popular masks toward larger personal realities. My patient signaled in her reflexive concern just such limitations.

For much of her life, image and concern had not seemed limitations but first-class tickets to popularity, success, the fast lane. Serving her image faithfully and serving just as faithfully those drawn to that image, she made herself vulnerable. It is the gap between image and reality on which the fact of vulnerability rests. Years ago I observed that as psychotic patients improve, their hallucinations are experienced as both closer to them and more friendly, until in the luckiest cases they merge into the voice of conscience and ideals. An Australian friend moved this observation in the opposite direction: some psychotic patients pursue their receding hallucinations so deep into the outback that they become lost and die. My patient's beauty image functioned like those fatal hallucinations. It was commanding because she served not only the image but the man she had drawn in pursuit of it. Serving him was dangerous in precisely the way disappearing into the outback is dangerous. He was pursuing something, an image, which in fact could not supply his real needs. As he became more deprived and desperate, her services had to become more frantic: the image had to be heightened and heightened again; her service had to be more and more abject and demeaning. They were moving farther and farther from any real source of supplies. Something like this happens in the most dangerous addictions.

Several times these sequences had climaxed in terrible quarrels and beatings; friends sometimes had literally torn the patient from the lover's embrace, once hiding her until the man disappeared. Other friends fed the process, baiting the man, demeaning her, loving to watch the beautiful people tear each other apart.

I wanted nothing so much as to give her a simple experience of being and, instead, found myself dreaming of romance. In this last we were together. She was in love with a difficult man and came to me unsure whether to leave him. I was unsure how to approach her. As I hold that time in my mind's eye, the two uncertainties mingle; I catch a glimpse of her agony and my nervous wish to help. Yet we were still miles apart. How important I felt at that time, so full of my mission and my image of her. How depleted I think she felt, by her uncertainty and her concern for me. In time we moved the image and concern away from our time together, to let her plight emerge. Her concern for me was slowly displaced by my concern for her. It wasn't easy for either of us. She was slow to feel worthy of a prayerful attention. I had the advantage of being in this place before, but what I gained from familiarity I lost to the still imposing image and my thoughts. As is common, we began with a misunderstanding characteristic of each of us, the image I formed and her concern. That is why every treatment is in part a treatment of the doctor, if only of his pretenses. You can feel my problems in the very telling of this tale. See how I shape it for my formula, the image and person suppressed. I had an image even of the process. How free was I, who meant to give her freedom?

Happily there are things I know to do. While I sat there wondering, I began to do them; they are second nature to me now. Because I am a psychiatrist I expected she would remember what other psychiatrists had said—would I agree? I knew her enthusiastic concern for others. I must relieve her of any concern for me. I wanted to clear our relationship of unspoken assumptions, expectations of behavior, everything that might impede our simply being together. I expected the impediments to appear one after another. I didn't want to argue about them or even discuss them. I wanted to flick them away. She mentioned that a previous therapist had diagnosed what seemed a grave condition. I said, "Oh my!" in a slightly mocking tone. Then, "We love to give ourselves important things to do." I saw no sure grounds for the diagnosis. Worse, there was no value in further burdening a self-deprecatory person. Frightening her into cooperation offered only short-term gains. Above all, I didn't want our relationship to sit in the shadow of an uncertain judgment: it was one more image to remove.

Also I didn't like her feeling so burdened with a need to help. Perhaps she felt that helpfulness justified her existence. I learned that she experienced it most of all toward her father, as her mother did. Again, pointing it out would only add to her self-dislike, indeed at a point she felt justifiable pride in. No, I wanted to relieve her. Being helpful toward her father, even toward me, might be useful (I knew I needed help). I just didn't want her to do it automatically, but to experience a relationship relatively free of images and expectations. This would also make it easier for her to recognize the automatic responses when they came.

She made me feel cared for. I meant to hand that back, to offset her concern. My awareness of her care immediately readjusted my response because that awareness carried with it a note of irony: what was she doing caring for me? I should be caring for her. The point is, I did not simply bask in it. Nor could I resent it, as a threat to my own sense of duty. I wanted my attitude to convey, thank you, how kind, but let me do as well for you.

All this supposes that I could convey an attitude by the way I sat, the tilt of my head, sounds I might make, the timing of responses. Words could hardly convey my set of feelings—the way my feelings set toward her. A verbal explication would itself, even if it approached musical accuracy, convey an intellectual, didactic attitude; it would require taking apart what I was trying to put together. Explaining would also speak to a part of her mind very likely engaged elsewhere, interrupted by the explanation. Better if she were to sense my set of feelings and respond to that.

Too much thinking and explaining would also distract our dealing with the outer world she faced. We don't treat in a vacuum; all the insights she might gain, all the changes in attitude or self-appraisal, would vanish if her world collapsed. She had a difficult boss and a difficult lover. How wonderful if I could arm her not only against myself but against them as well. Again, it had to be done economically, that is, sparing her and my energies. It was not to be like wheeling the whole army to a different front. So when boss or lover was referred to, I would take an attitude making clear what I felt about them. "Lord protect us," I muttered when the lover sang a fresh song or the boss waffled in his support. The idea was to line up support behind her as well as to warn; she would have me with her worrying about both these uncertain men. I also didn't want her work here with me to give a false confidence about life in the world. What might be settled here would not quickly settle there. I wanted the larger world and ours to mingle, just as I want the past not to preempt the present and future.

Psychotherapy always and usefully enters the past. At the start of the work, it can only do that safely if the present is attended to and a future is established. This is because looking at the past without a believable future risks despair. As the patient and I tried to find our way through typical misunderstandings and to stabilize her present, I looked for easy ways to touch that future. I wanted her to feel she had a guide watching the landscape of her life, noting points to guard but also promising sites or an interesting view. She should feel possibilities, not a great hope yet or a certain destination, but the fact of a future different from the present and past. "That may be something you do wonderfully well," I said about a project at work. "Be careful, you might make a career of it." The bleakest life hides moments of excitement and promise. Hers was far from the bleakest life.

I was making an inventory of our relationship, her present dangers, her possible hopes. I must do it quietly, unobtrusively, because she was not yet sure and free enough to use her own energy. The fact was that she would be eager to do too much. It was my job now. Her job was to receive, to practice with me that getting.

We were negotiating a different relationship. I wanted it simply to happen. By being what we were together, it could become a model for what she in turn negotiated with others, a new way of running her life. Each of us would learn fresh ways characteristic of being together. The wonderful solicitude she brought to so many might be a gift of her own freedom, not the chain it then was. And perhaps I could learn to hold my images lightly, wonder rather than know, speculate when I wanted to prove.

One day I was trying to sit with her and at the same time leave her alone. I wanted to give her the freedom to think and imagine independently of me. It could be an enlargement of her inner space; she could discover the right to talk or not talk without comment from me. Where should I look? If I stared at her, she would feel examined. If I stared too far away, she might feel ignored. So I tried to look relaxed and easy, not expectant and waiting. I let my own mind wander in the same way I wanted hers to. She began to speak in a low tone, as if to herself. She had always felt scrawny, ugly, unlovable; she worked night and day to replace that unbearable image by one of a moon goddess, a concert pianist, the president of every class. It was no use. The unbearable image seemed the reality; she could disguise herself but not succeed. Another therapist had called her a moon goddess, but he didn't seem real himself. She knew I believed in her, but that was no use either.

Look at the wonderful difficulty of my position. I had to disagree without being disagreeable. I couldn't attack or usurp her judgment, however wrong, because the reality of her existence was frail and narrow, little able to defend or even recognize itself, squeezed between an unbearable image and others attractive but unreal. I needed to be confident and light-hearted, gently putting her refusals to one side while my admiration shone. Reaching the real person suppressed is an act of imaginative belief that has to be felt. Happily I did feel both confident and light-hearted, almost certain that this real person would in turn shine forth. Meanwhile she turned on me in frustration and anger. "What use is this?" She accused me of taking from her what little she had and giving back nothing but emptiness. "How long will this go on?" I said, "Until you get back what you deserve, and your money's worth here too." She laughed.

I went on making my adjustments, honoring her separateness. The last lover didn't come around or, better, he came round and round. She showed in her response one quality that strengthened my belief in her. She wasn't like so many of us, loving the lover best after he or she has left. Her feelings were constant; they diminished as he diminished, a loss of size that accompanied his distancing but also his becoming trivial, backing and filling, not knowing his own mind, becoming, it seemed, the man he was. One of the hardest decisions I faced was how much to fight for him. I didn't want to side with her serving him, letting him have his way, however obscure that way was. Nor did I want her making a desperate pitch, serving herself up. In my heart I felt she should raise hell, shout out, "No one will treat me this way!" But she had to do it, not I.

She found the courage to confront the man and his wife, returning home at once shaken and intact. He didn't prove worthy of all she had invested. Now I was investing in her, which is to say I had faith and confidence. At first I suspect this confidence was as much her belief in me as it was mine in her, hers flowing out to me away from herself as it had done so many times before. Again, what I had to do was to replace her faith in me with my faith in her, a faith solidly based on my perceptions.

In medical school I volunteered to be a subject in an experiment on hypnosis. The hypnotic induction was begun, I felt myself becoming sleepy. Then came a command, or was it a command? "Your arm is rising." Indeed it was rising. I remember being puzzled whether "it" was rising or I was raising "it." I found myself in a territory between the voluntary and the involuntary, half slave, half free. My will and the hypnotist's had somehow merged.

At first the patient wanted to please me. I told her to shake the rafters. She did, awkwardly but willingly. Who was doing that? Then I might have said, "Do it on your own." "But how can I?" she could have asked—"When I know what you want me to?" I wanted to separate my will from hers and give her will a ground to play on, to develop and be celebrated. This would be a safe psychological place: she was buying it; now she could own it. There was a wonderful time when she began to humor me. I could feel her smiling behind the serious patient-hood of her bearing. She would not vividly yet make fun of me; she would not yet laugh in my face. But more and more I came to feel a strong independence, that very first-seen determina-tion, hovering behind the proper mask. I didn't want to seek it out, thereby perhaps frightening it back in. She still had to learn whether I could be trusted. There is, and was, no use saying "I can be trusted." Many are the patients who take a therapist's word for that and discover otherwise. Again there was no use talking about it: it had to happen.

Lucky parents sometimes overhear their children talking freely about them. They are wise not to let on. Better to contemplate the picture revealed, as a rule very different from the parents' conceptions of themselves. The conceptions must be different because the child, or any other person, stands in a separate place; each perspective is different. It is not only a matter of age or size or impulse; each person sees an individual world. Later on the young people may give a speech or write a letter in which they tell it their way. But at first it must be covert, often shocking. The shocked adult puts it down to immaturity; once it was godlessness. Many of us live in a little pool of feeling that we are generally liked, even loved, certainly not judged. The charge of immaturity or godlessness lets us return to that pool of feeling. I believe this delusion is far more common than its reverse, the conviction of being judged and disliked, which gets dismissed as madness and paranoia. It is hard to find where the truth is, though probably not at either extreme. I suspect that paranoids are closer than happy dreamers are. Having listened for a long time, I believe many of us should be thankful not to be shot.

Coming to life in one another's presence waits on courage and proofs of being trustworthy. There were no limits to what I had to discover about my own foolishness. Much later I showed a version of this portrait to the woman herself. She was very polite, very forbearing. I had many things wrong. For example, I made too much of my image theory and seemed bedazzled by romance. Nor was she ever so compliant as I thought. Between human caution, stubbornness, and our beloved theories, it is surprising we know anyone. Certainly it takes a long time. I sensed she had one of those powerful, even minds of broad reach. You meet that in leaders because leadership requires taking multiple perspectives, above all not losing perspective on what is great or small. Common sense should not be called that because it is common; the reverse is true. Common sense means separating the common from the uncommon, knowing what the best bet is, how the common run of things goes. She often made what proved to be wise calls at her place of business, not being easily distracted or misled. She had a gift for watching people's faces and being able almost to hear them think. She could see while many of the men around her chased phantoms. She didn't see herself so clearly. This took a long time, and it cost her dear.

One day she came in tattered and rueful. She had won a great battle at work. The men who employed her loved her image; it was everything an advertising agency could desire. And the concern and dependence behind it were just as desirable. All of this invited a corruption of power rarely resisted: she had to be a toy, a doll, a servant. It was her love life revisited at the office. The battle was fought on two fronts. The men fought to retain her image more fiercely than she had worked to create it. All the tricks that power knows—lovingness, surprise, brutality, sequestration—were thrown at her, that she should be as much a slave in the psychological sense as any manacled roadgang was to physical overpowering. It is the imposition of danger that power loves most, the threat of obliteration, an atmosphere just this side of doom: one more move and you're gone.

She could begin to see them for what they were, bullies, and herself for what she could be. Yet as bitterly as they bullied her, she bullied herself: here was the second front. To fight was to feel like them, to feel herself a bully. Such is the unconscious ally of every tyrant: power is made so hateful that the powerless cannot use it. This comprised the sharpest restriction on her freedom, as well as one source of her sweetness and concern, so that when she discovered her power, she became that much less attractive to many, including herself. She returned from her victory ashamed of herself. They had backed down, really fled, but now she felt like them. I could rejoice in the victory, congratulate her, celebrate, but she knew she had lost that image, not only of her serene and beautiful presence but of her ideal of service and concern. What was the compensation for that?

Henceforth she called herself a bitch, a word men like to use. It was as if she had gone over to the other side. Was that the compensation? It seemed to her more of a loss. I told her she was demeaning herself, that she was simply standing up for her rights, that if she raised her voice it was either because they were deaf or had already raised theirs. At one point I grew so vehement that she must have felt assaulted anew. I also wanted to tell her that she was using a word used for dogs and that a beloved dog had been her greatest compensation through many of these difficult times—she and the dog had loved each other. Madame de Stael is rumored to have said, "The more I see of men, the more I like dogs." I also felt the patient had led a dog's life without the protection some dogs get. I didn't say any of these things because they struck me as derogatory and I had grown more and more to admire her.

She called herself a dog. I wondered if she was not tempting me to join that charge. By chance I love dogs; I could join her in that. As I said, I also like to talk about the weather. When I was young, my father quoted Dr. Johnson as saying that only fools talk about the weather; most of them also like dogs. I didn't get off to an easy start. But in time I learned something. People who give room only to the brilliant and extraordinary misconstrue the ordinary. My father said he found the ordinary boring, when in fact it is often extraordinary, just as common sense is not common. Recall the old saying, speech is given to us for the purpose of concealing our thoughts, in this case shaping them according to one or another prejudice.

Stanley Cavell writes about Samuel Beckett's play *Endgame:* "Beckett's couples have discovered the final plot:

that there is no plot, that the truth has come out, that *this* is the end. But they would be mad to believe it and they cannot, being human, fully give up suspense. So they wait. Not *for* something, for they know there is nothing to wait for. So they try not to wait, but they do not know how to end" (*Must We Mean What We Say?* p. 132). I take this to mean that Beckett's couples are caught between the extraordinary and the ordinary, between a belief in plots and the whole persons suppressed. For a while the patient and I were caught there too, until things began to happen.

What appeared between us, and between her and others, was extraordinary despite its prosiness. She had described a series of problems on her job that seemed to me, and later to her, clear evidence of the boss's incompetence. Further, she had offered solutions to these problems, not once but many times, suggestive of her superior competence. She was disdained but they needed her, even now and then had sense enough to use her, though any large measure of such usefulness had to be forced on them. My point is that all this appeared between us in a continually moving way: it was at first sad, then redemptive, often ridiculous, more often suspenseful. And it was not only emotionally moving, but it was actually moving her toward both a greater authority and, as important, her and their acknowledgment of that authority. It became more and more difficult to take the boss seriously, a possible correction to his image as well. I didn't know if he was an ordinary Joe out of his depth or someone like her, feeling he had only the image of his title to go on and thereby forfeiting what might have worked, a little honesty. Notice too the changing focus and meaning of the "serious." She had not taken herself seriously, or she had taken seriously only her image and appearance, as the boss took his title. Even the demeaning treatment she received was not taken seriously until it issued in sickness and doctors. More and more the real came into view, as both their images faded, she more the boss and less the beautiful image, he more mindful of her ability and less full of his mock authority. In other words, images did not fall away to reveal a flat and featureless landscape but a landscape remarkably transformed. It took some getting used to. The real people had indeed been suppressed.

Still she felt like a bitch. In part the ordinary remained that, a dog's life. She didn't yet know her real beauty and strength and, I believe, others would not acknowledge them until she did. Part of her continued to feel that a force stood beyond her that was not simply powerful—this would always be true—but righter than she was, entitled. The images clung. I write this in some measure to persuade her, thinking that the printed word may do more than any spoken ones. Great people once had their portraits painted to exalt majesty. A few of them discovered what they really were; Clemenceau wanted Manet's picture of him destroyed. The patient did not ask that.

The best portraits seem to blend what is distinct with what is universal. You feel that in Rembrandt's pictures of himself. He loved to dress up, he had a red nose, there is something preternaturally wise inside those brown eyes—but most of him could be you or me. Perhaps that is why Borges has Shakespeare complaining to God that he always wanted to be himself and yet found himself being everyone, Ophelia, Macbeth, the fools, Lear, Falstaff. The patient played some parts herself and may find new ones. Also, she is wise and can trust her instincts. When she told me she feared becoming like the bullies, I said there was no chance: her sympathy would intervene first, if anything too soon. She might even have that rarest union of assets, gentleness and power. I always wanted her to be president of the firm, to take the job away from her boss. Maybe she will.

I felt self-indulgent. Perhaps she had produced that in me, as in many others. Then I remembered the dog and how he had supported her. Probably she looked forward to seeing him more than she ever looked forward to seeing me. And the man she married—he loved her with or without makeup, a good model for me. Of course they fought, as couples must, to establish a livable space. But besides spirit they both had loyalty, as vital as spirit in making that rare thing, a good marriage. Still only a fool predicts the fate of marriage; you can do better with the weather. Just wish them luck.

The long history of personal illusionment and disillusionment that Proust wrote provides in the end much the same story. The splendid aristocrats he had worshipped were consumed by the very envies and fears that nearly consumed the novelist in training; and the vocation of understanding and re-creation (in both senses, of art and play) compensated Proust for the fantastic world he had lost. He constructed a real world out of ordinary details, which, grasped, deepened, extended, were extraordinary indeed. It is odd to think that such an experience could be everyday.

2 ~ A Shy Acceptance

Narcissism is being in love with a perfect image of oneself. In many ways its opposite is depressiveness, which is being in hate with one's imperfect image. Collapse of the first regularly leads to the second. Narcissism also stands in contrast to such aspects of healthiness as accepting shortcomings, being open to and sober about their rediscovery, what has been described as "a shy acceptance" of our singular existence to which we have been both entrusted and exposed (Martin Heidegger, *Being and Time*).

Narcissism means not a shy acceptance but an enthusiastic entitlement to self-images of splendor, greatness, beauty, or paradoxically of modesty, even humility. We meet people brimming over with a sense of themselves, who cry out, "This is me!" What is a newfound joy in children and part of the experiments of adolescence defies reality in adulthood. It is the delusion of constituting oneself, of being the exclusive agent of one's own being.

Surely the existence is singular. A long experience of psychotherapy teaches the singularity of the most seemingly commonplace existences. Uniqueness does not do justice to what singular means: individual, private, peculiar to itself, distinguished, strange, odd, whimsical. The extraordinary resources of art and literature are mobilized to this depiction. But they fall short of what appears in nature. In fact artists cannot afford to desert their imagination and describe what really happened. No one would believe them.

It is an existence to which we are at once entrusted and exposed. It is mine to keep, but it is like keeping a bomb. I will describe a man whose existence had at least twice exploded, in a terrible accident and in his wife's sudden violence. I felt like an ordnance officer defusing a bomb. The acceptance can't be so shy after all: this is also mine to keep, protect, and control. Note the irony of "entrusted." This does not mean I can trust myself, no more than you can trust explosives. Long ago I learned for myself: I cannot do that. So I formed a cabinet of advisers and ran problems past the secretary of the treasury and the secretary of defense. No, it is entrusted *to* me, not because I can be trusted but because I know I can't be, and have taken precautions.

A handsome, slow-spoken man of fifty seemed the walking refutation of this nervous account of existence. You would have said, if I can't trust him I can't trust anyone, and you would have been right. He was an established lawyer, with a large, steady practice, a sociable dweller in a wealthy suburb, with a busy, pretty wife and two children. He could have been on a Norman Rockwell cover, except rumor had it that he was a loner and self-centered. I was also quickly puzzled about why he was not still better known and more successful; he had extraordinary qualities.

No one is excused from psychiatric patienthood, no more than there are built-in protections against surgery. Psychological vulnerabilities, times of up or down, are as universal as appendixes and more expensive. The good news is that you seldom die in the hands of your psychological helper, and you might come to life. But that would have all seemed irrelevent comment on a man so steady and grave. Why did he visit me? Perhaps the most symptomatic thing he did was not to explain it—suggesting that he saw himself very differently from the way he appeared.

I didn't ask him. His visit suggested that I should mind his business, but I was in no hurry. Maybe he was testing me. People do that a lot with psychotherapists, and wisely. Maybe he didn't know. He may have come because someone told him to, or he had heard something that moved him, or he was simply troubled and sought relief. Paul Cézanne is reported to have said that he was the landscape's consciousness: "The landscape is reflected, is humanized, thinks itself in me." Perhaps the patient wanted me to be his consciousness, wanted to think through me. I might even be able to do it, to help him find words for whatever was moving him, for whatever needed to be spoken or seen or be transcended. I might be a translator of a little-known tongue. I hope it is clear that most of what passes between patients and therapists as communication has very little reliability, just as the physical observations and information that passed between doctors and patients for many centuries were of the same small value.

For the most part, language does our thinking for us, and this man was a master of conventional language. It would be more accurate to say he was mastered by it. In all the time I knew him, I seldom heard him say anything confused or discordant. In the early Conrad (and the early Auden too), one feels that dissonance. Not only is Conrad learning to express himself in a new language, but his remarkable psychological intuition, his sense of reality, cannot be contained within any known language, straining and distorting conventional forms. By the time of the novel *Victory,* English had won. I miss Conrad's sudden glimpses of a perceptiveness startlingly novel.

There I was, sitting across from this capable man, wondering how to listen, how to talk. As usual, I wanted him to feel safe and to make contact, although beneath the smooth coilings of his mind and manner we watched each other warily. He said he had heard me speak ten years earlier and asked himself how real I was. I wonder that, too, and said so. Three years later, almost at the end of our time together, he said that two acquaintances told him they had always wondered how real he was. The patient felt changed, that they could tell him. In the meantime he had also begun to wonder how real his father was. Perhaps, at the very start, he had set the agenda, in the form of a question about me. And in acknowledging my wonderment, perhaps I had responded well. If I knew anything this man did not, it may have been just this commonness of the unreal. There was a happy paradox in the work: as he settled down in life, he shed the accepted inner structure of that life.

He had come from a distinguished Canadian family with a congenial sense of his and the family's soundness. There seemed no puzzles anywhere. The father had dominated the family by means of a powerful will and principles carefully articulated and endlessly announced. He was a philosopher and his family was the stage for philosophical demonstrations. The older brother, argumentative like the father, revolted early, never speaking to the father again. The patient was quieter, loyal, close to his mother. He exercised at most an occasional wry skepticism toward the father's convictions. The old man contrived to include that in his philosophical system.

The patient's success in the law of trusts and wills arose as much from his capacity to listen and identify with the needs of his clients as from his considerable intelligence and knowledge. People felt in good hands. It took me a long time to realize that he did not, that he felt himself always to be standing a little apart from the public image. This meant that a slightly pompous and self-centered manner noticeable to others was only now and then evident to the patient. His wife's complaints along these lines fell on deaf ears partly because of his unconsciousness but also because he felt safer in his pomposity, even a little proud, as if he had united himself with the powerful father. One sees here a principle basic to character. However obvious to others our impact, and however understandable in terms of our habitual actions, those actions are often opaque to us precisely because they are ours: we can't see them the way we see others, standing as we do within our own point of view. People who see themselves as others see them have, as an occasionally and happily broken rule, surrendered their points of view. But he liked his point of view, thought it either very sound or slightly outrageous but remarkable, like his father's.

Much is outrageous and potentially violent in any point of view that attempts to be more than just that, one of many perspectives on a mysterious and largely invisible world. The potential for violence arises not only from the need for some combative exclusiveness but also from an inner exclusiveness, a narrow self-definition, a love affair with some image of one's own. I believe this was what caused my patient his discomfort. For example, he often daydreamed, as people do, of having affairs. Proust said that nothing so isolates an individual as the practice of a secret vice. These imaginings were his secret vice and contributed to his appearance of aloofness. The discomfort came when these quite human longings and uncertainties struck against an equally beloved but less secret fantasy of what his life was—in particular, the focus of a perfect family and himself as the perfect father. The rigidity of that self-definition, its exclusion of wide-ranging imagination, threw him into conflict. This, to a psychotherapist, is the most comical aspect of secrets: we all breathe privately the same forbidden air. The patient, struggling both to express and to suppress shameful thoughts, confronts someone who not only has heard them before but has the same thoughts himself and suspects they are universal.

How was I to bring this proud and successful man to another point of view or, better, to additional points of view? I could confront him with my own, as his father had done, but then he might only acquiesce and revolt secretly. Even if I told him what I believed, that we all breathe the same forbidden air, it might make me into him in his eyes and not affect the inner image. I preferred to be the landscape's consciousness, to listen for other points of view within him, to let the fuller range of his humanity speak. It would also be a relief for him to know that freely imagining his affairs might save him from them, though he would not learn that until he had given more freedom to his imaginings. As it was, he had almost sleepwalked into several wonderfully compromising situations.

He often used an expression I have come to see as a signature of conventionalized experience. He would say Mr. Smith or Miss Jane was a "nice person." The point is that he said it as if he meant it, as if one could know such a thing or as if such a term describes any living being. This expressed the sharp distinction he made between convention and nonconvention, what he would sometimes refer to as "the weird." The same sharp distinction hobbled his mind. Thoughts were supposed to be sequential, orderly, appropriate. Anything else was a sign of weirdness, even madness. Because ordinary human thought is anything but sequential and appropriate, he couldn't let himself think very much; and when he did he was sure he must be nearly mad. I think this was the deepest reason he came to me: to clear up his thoughts, to cleanse him of the ordinary and the real.

Learning that we see things differently threatens our basic tribal unity. It invites a disrespect that reasserts our superiority. Disrespect also stands guard against the dreadful isolation springing from any keen awareness of a separate existence. As we struggle in psychotherapy to understand another's point of view, how a patient sees the world, that very struggle threatens the viewpoint's existence. "You mean there's another way?" Even the discovery of an illness does not challenge the viewpoint's integrity. But when I sit and wait to understand another, I assert our isolation and difference. No wonder psychotherapy is not everyone's cup of tea.

The work is only made possible by events that shake our comfort in the way we see things. Even a profoundly depressive outlook or its opposite, a boundless cheerfulness, escapes concern until events challenge the vision. It is like Thomas Kuhn's famous concept of scientific change: the paradigms of normal science preclude change until enough contrary instances force a shift. Even then a new consensus often waits for the young to get older and the old to die. The changes in my patient's point of view were hammered out of him, by violent events challenging his complacency. I felt what I often feel, that my largest task is to hold the patient while the blows fall, so that he can endure them, learn from them, not be maddened or broken.

Under cross-examination the defendant changed his story—the familiar line goes, "Yes, I was home that evening." So it was with my patient. He had come home one night to find every window in the house smashed. He was not so much stunned or panic-stricken, he told me, as wide-eyed. It was as if his personal windows had been forced open; only he couldn't see through them yet. He stumbled over his wife, drunk and sobbing. There was no telling the old story now: the perfect home with the perfect wife in the perfect suburb. Everybody a hundred yards around would know in the morning. He dragged his wife upstairs, comforted her a little, and then lay staring into the darkness. He said a streetlight made pretty patterns on the shattered window in front of him. She had been just as thorough in her breakage as she'd always been in her cleaning up.

He tried to remember if she had ever complained. He was thinking he should have been warned. He told me he had always felt he deserved her adulation and tirelessness, that she was somehow responding to him and he was then responding to her. Suddenly what they had been to each other, all man and all woman, felt uncertain, ridiculous. Then he said he closed that thought down, as if it were unworthy of all they had built together.

If anything had ever seemed weird in his life, it was the appearance of that house in the morning. There had been art in her drunken frenzy. She broke the windows with a shovel and then threw books and pictures out. It looked as if the house had exploded. He came upon himself in a large photograph, smiling up at a tree.

I thought it characteristic that he set about doing the right thing, family therapy, his own attendance at several meetings. And he took the advice he received very seriously indeed. There was a whole community of right-thinking people waiting out there to receive him and reregulate his life. I wondered if the wife would have to break all their windows too. It didn't sound as if she wanted to. She took up her new, chastened existence with the old enthusiasm. I felt a little like the proverbial bastard at the family reunion.

Yet for all the emergence of a new order, something besides glass had been shattered. He lost his sense of safety. The powerful father had given him that, through settled convictions, financial prudence and generosity, above all by having such a prestigious outlook to which the patient subscribed. The father gave him a coherent sort of selfhood that was almost everywhere confirmed by society, despite what a few others sensed of pomposity and aloofness. I felt like a spoiler for just this reason: the settlement, the seeming self-knowledge, the coherence of selfhood, even aspects of the new order, all struck me as illusions that must sooner or later come to grief against the facts of life. It is the matter of shy acceptance again.

"I know who I am and like what I am," he had proclaimed. He experienced his wife's frenzy as, "I don't like what you are and what we have become." She was unable to warn him, to tell him either before or after that night what was wrong. The alcohol released actions for which she never found words. The landscape, the consciousness of which I wanted to be, was suddenly broken and littered. He saw this new landscape and described it to me. Could it think through me?

Cézanne probably meant that his consciousness established relationships between parts of the landscape, brought its contrasts and uniformities into a sharper light. The artist was able as well to bring forth its beauty, which might be nothing more than what those contrasts and uniformities announced. We might say he gave the landscape meaning, if we had a clear idea of what meaning means. Most of all Cézanne saw himself as trying to be faithful to both the sensations of nature and the truth of the motif in front of him, to preserve his commitment to both what he felt and what he saw. (His point of view held those two elements in tension.) The resulting picture was inevitably his perspective. Its grandeur was to be measured by precisely the extent to which it was his perspective, because only by that individual depiction could the rest of us see what our points of view had not depicted. Only then could our points of view be changed, enlarged. It is the very individuality, the paradoxical fact of its being but one point of view, that gives the work its importance. It is the farthest thing from beauty in the abstract.

If I could get that littered landscape to think through me, I would be able to present it from my point of view. He would see how someone else saw it, this horror he could barely tolerate for even an instant. I could not describe it. I had not seen it. He had described it to me, and I could only respond to his encounter with it. Curiously, this being at second hand over and over convinces psychotherapists of an event's accuracy, a sort of sixth sense. Many a family member I have been able to feel, to depict accurately, by the measure of a patient's startled avowal. It is as if I can feel other persons' imprint on the patient, the form their feelings take on the patient. I don't guess how tall they are or the color of their hair, but how they feel. It is these feeling relations that constitute the emotional landscape.

He could barely tolerate that landscape because of the feelings it contained. Think of him as a terrified artist recoiling from the horror of a site not only seen (and described to me) but felt, as Cézanne himself so vividly felt the objects in front of him. Cézanne could be set in ferment by a bowl of fruit and transmit that ferment to us. The patient transmitted his ferment to me, really passed it through himself to me, so that I was able to experience more of it than he could. It was as if he were too close to the landscape not to be lost within it. And of course he was lost within it. It had taken him by surprise.

This illuminates the work. I must be able to face the landscape, his existence, for more than a moment. The cynical La Rochefoucauld claimed we all have strength enough to bear the sufferings of others. He was wrong. We recoil from the sufferings of others, at least from those sufferings that others present to us themselves. A therapist can say "thank God"—otherwise he would be out of business. The therapist also profits from another limitation of humankind. Each of us has only a particular perspective. However much we acknowledge other views, immerse ourselves in the world perspectives of art, religion, and science, we return to our solitary points of view. So in my "looking after" you, as the expression puts it, looking after you have looked, as at that littered landscape, I ask myself to seek and protect two existences neither one of us can fully know, because my own too must be safeguarded if I am to do the work. Only human desperation could find this a solution. Yet it escapes me how any other solution is possible, given the way humans are. That is, we need someone enough like us to share our feelings and different enough to have a separate perspective. I must be able to get on the human ground and yet stand in my unique human spot, and every spot is unique. It is like going on a picnic: you want someone else along but not a bear or a lizard.

No doubt he was often unsure of what I was, perhaps a bear or a lizard, and I had the same doubts about him. I wondered, for example, whether he or his wife might not be male and female impersonators. I don't mean that, if they took their clothes off, each would have the other's genitals. (That has happened, but it didn't seem likely here.) I only wondered if they were really so much man and woman. It was perhaps a measure of their loyalty to conventions, of their not only speaking but believing the language they used, that they spoke of themselves as man and woman. Here the meaning of meaning is clear. They meant it. The meaning of their being, their identity, was constituted by these familiar words. The words felt like rafts flung out to otherwise uncertain people in an uncertain sea. The words seemed to say: however unconstituted I am, this I know. It may seem a contradiction in a man so firmly constituted that he needed to make such a statement. But such is the nature of those beloved self-images; they have to be asserted and reasserted again, just as the narcissist loving himself wants you to love him too, because in fact they are only images.

Not just common usage but a universal belief says the opposite: I *am* a man, I *am* a woman. Androgyny is an aberration. Anatomy is destiny. I have my beloved sperm, my testicles, my penis. Are these not evidence enough? Some gay men, worshipping maleness to the point of being able to love only other men, say it even more firmly. They are not too different from men similarly worshipful who can love no women not worshipping their maleness. Perhaps only the pubescent youngster, sometimes feeling himself or herself (which is it to be?) teetering between identities, knows the plain truth: these words, man and woman, male and female, refer to physical facts and psychological states seldom if ever purely one or the other.

It was the tribal conventions of difference that my patient worshipped. They had been struck down from both within and without. His neighbors could not have been more surprised had he changed his gender. Some of the neighbors may have felt safe too and wondered whether their homes could explode as his did. I have seen such events ripple through close communities. Of course I was concerned about his safety. On what basis could he place his existence, once the idea of a normal or even superior person or family had collapsed?

Henceforth his acceptance of the life he led became a great deal shyer than it had been, if we mean by *shy* wary or diffident. The old pleasure in his ways could reassert itself only gradually and in the absence of further explosions. These I wanted to prevent. My hypothesis was that he had been exercising over his family, in fact over his whole existence, a subtle, pervasive censorship based on confidence in his way of seeing things. His wife colluded in this from what I felt was uncertainty about her own point of view. Now, like her, I wanted to open windows.

My method was to be his landscape's consciousness. This meant listening for contrasting signals that might animate the old monotonous scene. It meant scanning the person and his existence, always avoiding intentness on one part alone. I was to be like those hearing aids that pick up background noise. It meant displacing the patient from the central and overpowering location he held in the picture of his existence. The painter needs to balance one great oak with other features of the landscape perhaps differently colored and shaped. He must let a great deal more come in. The patient would decide what to keep, but he needed to feel the more interesting variety and vivifying conflict that such an openness provides. The single-minded image might fade.

What I tried to do was this: amplify signals otherwise faint or quickly suppressed. I wanted to bring forward as much as I could, integrate as much as I could of what was suppressed or forgotten. A great deal, I'm sure, escaped me behind the careful, steady, logical course he held to. It helped, I believe, to create a sense of admiring more about him than he admired. He took an ardently pathological attitude toward some of the best parts of himself. In this he would have done honor to the most mordant of psychoanalysts. It is a sad fact that pathological concepts are very easily pressed into the service of stultifying conventionality.

As I said, he viewed disconnections of thought, especially novel or surprising disconnections, as signs of madness. He was slow to see them as possibly creative or indicative of what was particularly his. Hostile feelings toward other people were perhaps the most forbidden of all his mental events. One of his father's precepts had been the absolute destructiveness of personal rage. The inevitable orneriness of so many of us renders this a troublesome family rule, especially in the absence of opportunities for professional mayhem. I am no great fan of personal rage. I have suffered enough from it within myself and from others. But there is no value in pretending that it is not a regular visitor to mental life. Again, a shy acceptance of a singular existence would have served him better.

The largest way in which I became part of his landscape's consciousness was by simply being there. I took up my spot in front of and slightly to the right of him. Earlier I said that my having a point of view inevitably challenged the exclusiveness of his own, which was accentuated by the fact he attributed to me, an older man, an authority that was like his father's point of view. In this way he tried to occupy my perspective, familiarize it. All the while he knew I was not his father, so that the way he saw how I saw was split and contradictory. This served my purposes well, particularly the purpose of experiencing and acknowledging the universally contradictory nature of humankind. The fact that we spent such a small part of our lives together also feathered my arrows, gave them a relatively direct line of flight that a more diverse acquaintanceship would have dissipated. We were together for a purpose at once definite and indefinite, limited but possibly without end. Again the paradoxical and self-reflective aspects of human functioning were highlighted. There was nothing else we could do except look at each other, reflect, and look out at the world together. Moreover, I secured a sort of local charisma from being depended on and paid, most of all from being constituted judge and jury. To some measure a patient inevitably puts his existence if not in the hands of the therapist then certainly in his mind, where it has to be judged. Whatever intellectual neutrality we can manage, there is never an emotional neutrality. In fact what the therapist experiences as neutrality often seems to the patient an indifference, which can be more corrosive than hate. I was now part of his landscape as well as an instrument of its consciousness, so that if he asked me what I thought, part of that landscape would speak. Here was another shattering.

In reflecting on each other, in wondering who and what we were for each other, the shattering both continued and evolved into a process of resettlement. I hope I have conveyed that he was a man wonderfully equipped for life. His very intransigence, his seeming to know and delight in what he thought he was, included a capacity to be someone; he had reached that self-delight of childhood and adolescence. It was no great step from image to the whole person suppressed. The start of his shy acceptance was at first more a wariness of me than of himself. I felt to him like his father, capable of mighty pronouncements. But there was the split in this perception: I didn't look like his father, and above all I didn't sound like his father. The contrast made the memory of his father clearer. In addition, it served to separate him from the father through his hope that I would be kinder and more reflective. The father was moving away from him in the changing landscape, the feeling relationships, of his mind. It seemed as if that movement separated him from a grand power just when he was emerging as his own person.

Or did it only seem that way to me because there was a new grand power invisible to my perspective because I was that power? Therapists, with that local charisma, easily creep into the minds of patients and exist there like tumors, even supportively, until disappointment or disappearance turns them malignant. I could console myself with the possibility of being a more benign tyrant than his father may have been, but surely that is the consolation of every tyrant. In fact I wanted to be a liberator, not a tyrant. What assurance was there of that?

It comes down to the old puzzle. How do you give someone freedom? Don't they have to take it? Don't they have to wrest it away? Didn't he have to break my windows? Here I was, his hired servant, trying to keep up my practice, hoping to be a liberator, but in some ways a despot. On the one hand he needn't break my windows; he could fire the hired servant and march out my door. On the other, there I sat in his landscape, sometimes larger than life. Again he was like that proud adolescent. He could walk out the door, but what would he take with him? I might become even more powerful.

It is the presence of both these elements, the power and the helplessness, that fuels the liberation. If he was to outface me as his father, he needed to know I depended on him for my livelihood. If I was to give him life, he needed some of the same power over me. So it was. He knew his power. Many lawyers have relationships with their clients not so different from therapists'. And he was an astute observer. He could appreciate the central role his wife had played in shattering conventions; he could begin to do for her what she had done for him, open the way to a voice of her own. He could also be my landscape's consciousness, Hour by hour he became more direct, accurate, and funny as he reflected on the existence before him. He was especially good on my pomposities, my doomed love affair with myself. We shared a lot of ground.

3 ⁓ Failure and Tragedy

One purpose of psychotherapy is to avoid tragedy. For all its hopes of individual development and fulfillment, therapy stands against tragedy. The failure I put at the head of this chapter is a failure of psychotherapy. I look back on it with persistent regret, asking myself what I could have done differently, because learning is the chief consolation we find in such events. This chapter is also part of a personal compensation process by which I exchange images of infallibility for the awful truth.

In some definitions tragedy is what no one can prevent—it is fate or character or context—so that psychotherapy is again what some still consider it, an impudence, futile and unnecessary. In fact, when therapy defeats tragedy, their opposition measures the passion required for success and the pitilessness of the tragic alternative. That the work can also be futile will be evidenced by the outcome I describe: the mad may not learn they are mad or the honest that they are honest or the dishonest that they are dishonest. Sometimes psychotherapy commands the passion to discard blindness, this seizing on an image of oneself. King Lear cried out, "Who is it that can tell me who I am?" It can be very hard.

I have never treated a king, even an abdicated king, but I have tried to treat the successful. That is very hard too. Give me the down-and-out any day; they know they need you. My tragic patient had a mind of such brilliance and determination that it could secure her views on any subject with the same ingenuity and fervor that had led her to revolutionize a branch of architecture. And what made her views still more strongly, almost palpably, held was their balance; competing interests were locked in an embrace I could not break.

There will be a temptation at the end of the chapter to claim I did not fail. Perhaps the death this remarkable woman chose was right; no other way may have lain before her. Certainly she did not act blindly, as far as I can reconstruct. Maybe she died the way the heroic brave die, caught between a love of life and a love of idea. I don't know. But I do know it is the glory of healing of whatever type never to accept that judgment as final: to search and search, so that future life has its best chance.

Whether failure or not, I believe this outcome illustrates the relationship of tragedy and character and context; these are as close as life gets to fate. I could not stop her from doing what she always did; and I could not stop those around her, including myself, from responding with the same consistency. We were like planets locked in orbits.

"Once upon a time, in the far-off kingdom of . . ." So the story goes: the right start for this tale of spells, enchantments, trials, about people of royal attainments, with only the ending wrong. What part did I play, a failed Merlin, Polonius, Rumpelstiltskin? And is my story what happened at all? Did I invent it, out of bits and scraps of what happened, for reasons of my own? Right up to the end I thought it would turn out right, although my energies had begun to flag. Why wasn't I more frightened, not raise a louder alarm? I did raise some, but my general confidence suggests blindness, self-deception, danger.

As I have said, telling the story is a process of compensation, the exchange of complacency for existential angst. To learn from the story I have to discover something in it I didn't know at the time, or something I didn't believe enough to act on. I have to discover that I was taken in, that the enchantment included me. But there is a catch. I want to tell the story so that it will come out right, in the sense of teaching something, to make up for the way it turned out wrong. Can I now tell it as it was? In the long run, and the run may not be long enough to settle the issue, the truth of what I may have discovered will only be known by its results in action: that I don't make the same mistakes again. It is an experimental proof, except that I can't arrange the experiment.

I am obliged to consider every possibility I know how to consider. I must look for signs of any disease productive of an unbearable mood, or the patient's character and effects, the effects of her powerful lovers and friends, my effects and all the interactions of these and other factors. The good doctor does not consider only his pet causes, be they diet or exercise, viruses or trauma. Medicine in its beginnings, as for example Robert Burton in his *Anatomy of Melancholy,* made incredible lists of possible causes: the weather, rain in particular, foxes, eating fish. Some have not retained their interest, but many more have been added—and psychiatry is new at this. So I can't tell the story right. I expect my account will seem as ludicrous some day as Burton's does now. But tell the story we must. And it is not we but I who tell it. That puts me in the ambiguous position Proust ascribes to the intelligence: intelligence may not be as important as feeling or instinct, but only intelligence can say so.

I begin by describing her not only because she was both patient and victim but because she was most prominently *there.*

It always surprises me that everyone looks different. Why aren't there more who seem duplicates of one another? (I grew up looking for them on the subway in New York.) But she took the cake. Only she could have given ugliness and awkwardness worse names than they have already. Yet this remarkable woman was as lovable as she was ugly, and her intelligence simply shone out, direct and magical. One imagined her able to do both the noblest and the most perverse things in the world.

The contrasts, of ugliness and luminosity, intense forwardness and pathetic humility, bespoke an astounding range of abilities and passions that were as various as they were unsettled. She was at once the relentless engine of her destiny and a baseball in the world series, at one moment clear, systematic, incisive, at the next prey to appalling dreads. The psychotherapist has to be a master of feelings in the same way a surgeon masters tissues or an internist chemicals. I watched this kaleidoscope—how much did I ever master it? It was real, felt, present, not acted or imagined. But where was wholeness? The range was there, but where the person to contain it? I wonder if I ever admitted that to myself.

She came to me in chaos. The wonderful work she had done was not yet appreciated. She was separated from her husband, while a new man alternately charmed and insulted her. Above all she never seemed to rest: there were projects, speeches, children, other lovers; she seldom said no. For all of a decade my efforts went on in a whirlwind. Her work became triumphant, with even more challenges and demands. She settled, more or less, in one relationship; the quarrels continued. She had been hospitalized before I knew her—once in the first year of my time; most of the decade she was on two or three of a half-dozen medications. Neurologists, psychologists, and chemists could find nothing conclusive to do.

I found plenty to do, keeping upright in the whirlwind. We never settled. I would say we never created a life if she had not been so full of life and her life so full of everything. Incidents, victories, celebrations, new projects, and real deepenings of her professional efforts succeeded one another relentlessly. Still, what I have come to hope for did not happen: the removal of such incidents to the background of life while something more ordinary and human comes forward. The subject of Proust's great novel is the novel itself, how after all the illusions and disillusions of life the act of re-creation redeems what had once seemed suicidally hopeless. All the fantastic promise and excitement of that young man receded into the background while his reflectiveness, his intuitions, the man himself, came forward. Psychotherapy, too, hopes to use these illusions and disillusions to create a life. Life was the source of Proust's work; his work was then the source of his life. In the same sequence, life streams into the therapeutic situation and then, sometimes, becomes the source of a new life. One wants to create one's life, as Proust did. Could she and I do that?

One of the largest enemies I faced was her success. It captivated me. I believe this was one of the principal ways I interfered with her development. The image of that success held me, stood between her and me, stopped the recession of incident, triumph or tragedy, into the background and our ordinary presences from emerging. This plagues the health of the successful as much as the reinforcements of success. When I admire you because you are bright and beautiful or talented, I interfere with simple being. The interference occurs most poignantly in the suspicion that "you only like me for one reason."

My theory about the patient's tragedy is just this failure of being, our inability to reach it. What would it have meant for us simply to be together? Her busy mind or, alternately, her despair and dread needed to find a resting place . . . in what? I begin to say interest, concern, hopefulness, but each of these involves itself too deeply in some particular ability, danger, or aspect of the future. Each resists a mindfulness that simply attends on her. That is to say, I felt too distracted to provide a resting place.

Even now my anxiety moves me ahead of the story. It didn't seem uncertain in the beginning; then there was hopefulness and a sturdy setting to the work. She had just come out of the hospital, her work status was in danger, there was an inhibited fury at her helpers and a great sense of isolation, even a need to retreat further. But with all this I was at home. Despite her despair, she was lively, challenging; the very range of difficulties invited action across a broad front; there was much at stake. I wanted my enthusiasm and confidence to offset the defeats she had suffered and the ones still threatening. The enemies she felt surrounded by, the precariousness of her professional position, the lovers and friends she felt had abandoned her—all these were to be taken on, with me beside her. She must not apologize or sneak away.

Our victory was not rapid, but it was complete. The enemies retreated or became accomplices; her professional position was stabilized and then vastly improved; lover and friends, if they must seem henceforth less certain, were no longer abandoning—they signed right up. Once demoralized, she was now remoralized, and very grateful. It was as if King Lear were back on this throne.

I was not allowed to forget, however, that this was no single battle but a war, a ten-year war. Early in her career she had worked closely with an engineer who became, like her, a leading figure in his field. They had a romance, then a bitter falling out; the credit and payments for several projects were left unsettled. Litigation began, was postponed, and finally re-opened when my patient's other commitments made a decision necessary. What followed was a skirmish that could have been a model for the whole war.

She went to court with her attorney, sat down with the old partner, and then gave everything away. As far as I can tell, he bullied her into it. The attorney protested, and he was bullied. It was not simply a defeat: it was a ruin; she gave away her home, her savings, a large part of her income. She became demoralized again.

Again I counterattacked. The lawyer was replaced, by one who could out-bully Hitler, and over two years the lost property and money were regained. A sort of stability was achieved from which she mounted a new array of projects and engagements. Yet something more fundamental was missing. The patient regained possession of her worldly goods but not of herself. Had I learned the corollary lesson: if she was not in possession of herself, could someone else be?

In what sense do any of us possess ourselves? We certainly talk as if we possess our children, but how do we possess ourselves? We are early possessed, not only by our parents but by fashions, friends, hopes, fears. Then responsibility means only the ability to respond. To possess ourselves there must be someone to possess and someone to do the possessing, a latter someone who transcends drives, habits, defenses, diseases. The easiest way, I believe, to determine if such an agency, person, or self exists is to notice if this self can protect itself. There are generous souls who wish to give themselves away out of piety or principle, perhaps in the service of a deeper self-enhancement. But can the self protect itself when it needs to?

Psychic health requires both freedom and compliance—the ability to connect and disconnect, to connect with others and to leave and protect oneself from others. It is like nutrition, which depends on both eating and not eating, as anorexics and bulimics discover. There is implicit separateness, that you and I are not the same, that each of us has motives very difficult to discover and at times very important to discover, that we both need to be with each other and to be apart. Every attempt to be without either society or solitude founders on this double demand.

My patient could not protect herself against the aggrieved partner, protect even her basic assets, because she did not feel they were hers. There was a hint of this in the way she dressed, an indifference that was more than eccentricity or rebellion. It was as if the physical boundaries of her presence were diffused or unknown; there was no demarcated, clad person. Only in the region of her ideas did one sense ownership and the capacity to protect. An acquaintance said it: she seemed a walking, speaking set of ideas.

Learning self-protection meant claiming other elements as her own, owned by her. She could have been a saint in her indifference to worldly goods. I suspect her tragedy sprang in part from this indifference, which extended to her feelings as well. What I mean is that I never heard her say or imply: you hurt my feelings. It was as if they were not *her* feelings, that she had no right to insist on their being treated right. She could feel crushed, but she did not, so far as I could tell, feel invaded. That suggests a boundary others are not supposed to cross; she lay open, like a province or a colony belonging to someone else. One other aspect of her feeling life was equally dangerous. She was not only unprotective, but she gave herself away. I like to quote Hilaire Belloc's cruel lines about the politician Godolphin:

> Today I heard Godolphin say
> He never gave himself away.
> Come, come, Godolphin,
> Scion of Kings,
> Be generous in little things.

My patient was generous in very large things. She gave freely of her time, money, often her ideas. Belloc implies that Godolphin's self is small, probably nasty. Whatever inadequacies my patient's self contained, I never knew it to be small or nasty. For all the meanness with which she was often treated, she did not respond meanly.

Giving yourself away is a phenomenon related to wearing your heart on your sleeve. But the former implies an active process, generally an involuntary process, more conspiratorial than simple nakedness. Later in this book I will examine nakedness as a psychological phenomenon, its dangers and treatment, but here I address something more hazardous. In friendship we also give ourselves away; that is its joy and its peril. True or safe friendship implies that the one to whom the gift is given cherishes and protects the gift. The openness and closeness of friendship are not then violated. When I offered these speculations to my patient, she didn't know what I was talking about; even when she finally "got it" her perilous adventures continued. I never persuaded her of the danger she was in.

Sometimes her "friends" quite literally took possession of her by means of what she told them. One particularly wrenching example occurred soon after we began. She told a colleague some of her dreads. The colleague assumed she was mad and suggested to the head of her firm that she be put on medical leave. The colleague's possession of her came about at the request of the boss. The colleague was asked to look after the patient, which meant an almost constant scrutiny. My patient acquiesced in this because she was still demoralized. Indeed, she encouraged her keeper's scrutiny with expressions of gratitude. An extensive consensus developed around the theme of her incompetence, with many people basking in their helpfulness of this well-known person and the patient trapped in her thankfulness. One of the ironies was that the "mad" person went on very effectively and creatively designing an important project.

The tragic possibility was here foretold, I now think, in this combination of strong figures competing to possess her, the great ability maintaining itself amid apparent devastation, and nothing like a simple relationship to help claim the person at risk. Worse yet, as the years passed and crisis succeeded crisis, I became only another of the competing, basking forces tearing her apart. And the dim perception I had of the work still undone faded with what I fear was simple exhaustion. I think she killed herself because she perceived nothing in her future but this same tearing, the division of her among warring parties.

What would I do if I had it to do over again? As I said, I was captivated by the image of her success. I needed to find my way past that to the person behind. Also I didn't yet grasp what

I illustrate in the next chapter—how to move a relationship to a more protected place.

There was a moment near the end when she spoke to me of friendship, how it seemed to have fled. Her once closest friend had died, two others lived far away. She had students, a lover, colleagues, but no friend. Then she looked straight at me. I sensed her meaning, but only in part. I thought she meant what is called socializing, having dinner together or taking a walk. That was stupid. The meaning of friendship doesn't spring from its setting or occasion. It springs from the nature of its psychology, what it does for you and me. It was a certain kind of supply she needed, again the contents, not the package.

She needed to be at ease and yet not alone, not fought over, not defended, even not understood. All the descriptions I know of this place and its purpose leave me dissatisfied, so let me try my own. Note that I venture here outside disease theory or the psychoanalytic model of mental functioning on the basis of drives and defenses in which there is at best an unstable equilibrium. What I want to describe is a psychological place in which individual viewpoints play but do not quarrel, are separate but not alone.

The hardest part to understand is the not-knowing, the removal from this aspect of the work of any effort to penetrate, formulate, cogitate. The great engine of theory and search Freud set in motion was fueled by his extraordinary intellectual reach and curiosity. Words poured out of him, onto pages and pages that clarified and explained. The relationship between analyst and analysand was little more than a moment in the great river of a general psychology flowing into medicine, literature, art, history, religion, almost everywhere. The patient's having to be a moment in that movement shadows the work, controls as it illuminates. "Have you been analyzed?" the observer asks. "Have you partaken?"

But if we set aside understanding in the intellectual sense, what does one do? We are not now waiting to hear. An expectant silence makes demands on the other, starts a little meter of revelation and accomplishment. I like to say, following Robert Frost's description of the poet's stance, that I am waiting for something to occur to me, not to the other. The point is, it should come of its own. Yet that is not enough to say either. Not everything that occurs to me belongs between us. I have to pass that occurrence through a mindfulness of you and me, to see if it feels all right, to see if it will play. By play I mean sit lightly between us, and allow us parts to play, to exercise ourselves, in this coming to be.

What would it have required for us to do that? Earlier I remarked on the extraordinary balance of her views; competing interests seemed to look each other in the eye, each moving to the rhythm of the other. Her architectural constructions had the same fearful symmetry, though often disguised or even abated. She could do nothing for one without giving something away to another. It was as if Emerson's compensation principle was hers to administer. There was no waiting on chance or justice or retribution; all these she delivered. She played God. Or rather God played her, because the compensation principle was not hers in the sense of being freely chosen. Like her impulses, surrenders, and dreads, the need for balance seized her, and she was powerless. I could throw myself in the balance here and there, pleading for mercy or leading a charge. What was needed, I think, was entirely different. It was nothing less than a revolution. The forces previously in charge—impulses, principles, fears, rapidly following each other in office, like an unstable republic—had to be overthrown.

The process by which a coherent self emerges has prompted some of the most interesting speculations of our time. I especially cherish the idea that both impulse and principle have to surrender their authority to something called *me* and *mine;* both impulse and principle have to be acknowledged and then owned or disowned. What makes this speculation interesting is its simultaneous defiance of body and god: it is neither biology nor theology, but psychology. Moreover, the speculation flies in the face of much that eastern psychology teaches about the essential transience and ineluctability of the self, the self existing somewhere between here and nowhere.

In order to save her, I had to find or create a person that was no longer pulled apart, a self that owned her warring impulses and prohibitions. Recall the patient's opposite, the complacent lawyer who created a seamless world, unpenetrated by new ideas or different viewpoints (even by the idea there is another viewpoint), carrying the individual from one moment to another on the smooth tracks of established beliefs, until it was all shattered. In contrast, my patient grasped other viewpoints as easily as if they were hands held out for her to shake. This was a major source of her disorganization: she could listen to those viewpoints, even extend their own arguments, be possessed by them. Where many people cannot imagine in detail how someone can disagree with them—or if that state is approached, steadily downgrade the disagreer to stupid, bad, at the bottom mad—she would elevate the other, often to the point of ruling her beliefs.

The shaky openness of her person also facilitated her originality. Ideas that could not penetrate more conventional spirits were either welcomed or seemed to bubble out of her like steam and lava from volcanic ground. Carl Jung said of James Joyce and his psychotic daughter Lucia—whose startling letters and speech Joyce thought resembled his own writing—that they were like two people going to the bottom of a river, only one was diving and the other falling. But in fact every dive is at least somewhat a fall, and the same is true of falls. The patient sometimes dived and sometimes fell.

The so-called normal self needs to be opened to new ideas and other perspectives, lest it be caught unprepared and stay unsympathetic. The architect needed to be less sympathetic. It was also true that nothing could surprise her, since the incidental and the catastrophic had an equal hold on her emotions. She needed surcease, peace, if only the "normal" person's peace of complacency. In the end she had to find it for herself.

She went on giving herself away, stripping off that discretion with which wisdom clothes the self. She found a new love, promised eternal devotion, was pulled back by another, watched the collapse of one project, found herself savagely attacked for another, promised too much of herself to a third. Knowing how desperate she was, I persuaded her to enter a hospital. She ran away and shot herself.

This tragedy is a failure of our relationship because one way, sometimes the only way, these escalating sequences can be broken is in a relationship. I have often seen it happen. One builds, in the intensity of the mutual regard, a place where desires can be expressed, ideals weighed, and the self provided its cement. Then the psyche, self, soul (how troubled we are even in its naming), for all its elusiveness, its subjectivity, its being at once subject and object, and almost not to be experienced, does in fact make a reality.

Imagery

In *The Varieties of Religious Experience,* William James addressed an old mystery. How are the saints, with their visions, voices, and odd behavior, to be distinguished from mad people? Hallucination and possession, tremblendem and mysterium, the sense of great external power, shifting in helpfulness and responsibility—these unite the two. Both have also been called adaptations, though some would term them maladaptations. Both have been claimed to mark the breakup of old patterns, the search for new ones; indeed by the success or failure of that search, many workers have distinguished morbid from religious solutions. James thought that what distinguished victory from defeat was the emergence of "that by which men live," ideals or aspirations that center the self amid the conflicting demands of inner and outer life. It is only by this means that one can say no to some demands instead of no to life altogether. Yet in this there is also a paradox that illuminates tragedy. Tragedy can be a clinging to an image of oneself that forbids ordinary life. For her it was an image of extraordinary fairness, of an equal weight to all the forces impinging that left too little for herself. I could not help her find a life of her own.

4 ~ Some Gestures

If the self is elusive, the connection between selves is even more so. Sealed within our perspectives, we catch a glimpse of life and resolve to change our ways. The resolutions pile up, the careful lists and careless hopes, but little happens. Or, better, any change we experience simply happens, apart from the resolutions and hopes. Sometimes these changes seem the result of attitudes we take toward one another, often expressed in gestures and movements, such as the mixture of concern and irony I felt toward the woman with the chestnut hair. I believe it was this way with the quiet woman in the episode about to be recounted.

One day she awoke, went to work, and around noon remembered that all morning she had not wanted to die. She told me it was the only morning in memory that she had not wanted to die. I was as surprised as she was, for the opposite reason. She came upon hope, and I came upon her despair.

I didn't think I knew her at all until she made a gesture the third time we met. Until then I don't remember ever feeling more at sea. She said almost nothing, was polite and friendly, greeting and parting, didn't treat me so much as a piece of furniture as another piece of furniture, like herself. I in my sixties, she in her fifties, we sat around, like the chairs and tables, inclined a little this way or that, until the gesture.

It came out very gradually, like the opening of a flower. At first I imagined it was one of those obscure greetings young people make to each other: passwords in a secret society. Then it seemed odd, the way some people smile at nothing in particular. Finally, I thought she was taking her time. She had sat for a while; perhaps now she was starting to look around. She never tried to socialize, to conventionalize our meetings. She just let them develop. It seemed I had passed whatever test she set for the safety of our relationship. I had let her alone. That might be why she made the gesture.

The reader of these pages may already have been frustrated by a lack of defining details that round out a story or anchor it in some fact. Or you may have sensed these are not stories, with beginnings, middles, and ends, because all such stories must be imposed on lives about which a great many stories can be told. Nor are any facts final, except for some story chosen as the best one. This was true of the quiet woman. Previous therapists had told different stores about her, and new facts, including the fact of her creative imagination, were always coming to light. The point is that I did not want to impose a story or pick one out. I wanted to see if there was a useful attitude I could take in the happier, slight deflection of a life that had its own momentum.

I wanted to make our relationship work. The way it worked, or didn't work, would be the only reliable knowledge I could ever have about her. Everything else would be secondhand; even her reports about herself could only be partial, for we are all partly strangers to ourselves. From long experience I have concluded that making a relationship work can be carried out into the world to make life work for the individual so treated. Such a treatment is less a curing than a learning to live, and less a learning to live than the making of a few corrections to habitual movements in order to encourage purposes often already in place. It is like the treatment of the body—most of the body works well, but here and there something needs to be done.

Her gesture, my attitude. She had relaxed, turned her face more toward me, creating the merest impression that could have been a figment tossed up by my hoping imagination. So I did nothing, lest I presume. Then she spoke, or rather whispered. This tall, strong-faced person appeared suddenly smaller, hidden. She said she felt far away. Again I didn't make much of this because, if she felt far away, I may have been too close and responding quickly might put me closer. I wanted her to find a comfortable distance, a good space in which we could get along.

My first response was little more than a slight movement toward her, immediately checked by a fear of intruding. It reminded me of how I feel when I start to write. There is an eagerness to begin before anything specific has occurred to me. I reach fearfully. Then I draw back, knowing how futile this is, and I wait. I keep my general subject in mind, but I have to wait. If significant and natural words are to happen, they just have to come up from the countless impressions germinating inside. The response I await gathers from within and announces itself by being unexpected. Previous, partial movements will be flicked aside just because they are expected, because they are platitudes. But with the unexpected one must hurry to catch up.

The unexpected inner movement created in me was a feeling of the patient's fragility; she was desperately in need of honor and protection, but the natural right to claim such things had quite disappeared from her mind. I felt she won't ask for anything; to demand is at the opposite end of her universe, and I can't demand for her because that is so remote. My gestures felt both toward her and away, honoring and shying all at once. It was a feeling of impossibility corresponding to the conflicting impulses that occurred to me.

To be rightless in a world where the concept of rights, if not the reality, is widely proclaimed, to be without free thought, much less free speech, in a world resonant with a cacophony of protesting voices—is that possible? Yes, because a vast space separates public rights and expression from the inner world that is so often silent and faceless. What is assumed, heralded, legalized, can vanish inwardly toward an unbending sovereignty in which every thought and action is controlled. She had said she felt far away. I responded, if one can call my timid movement a response. But we were not engaged, barely present, groping in the dark.

Imagine living with a watchful tyrant who is not just nearby but within your own mental space, in fact occupying more of the space than you do, so that feeling far away means you have been pushed to the periphery of your own existence. Worse, you are awed and self-reproachful, to the point of identifying with and even revering the power. Many such powers are remorselessly critical, and as insiders they are privy to any protesting thought. The result is a level of control unimaginable in the most tyrannical police state.

How can the patient be freed? The answer lies in a similar vulnerability of the police state. Recently we have watched one such state after another collapse, states once thought invincible. Their vast, intrusive, torturing machinery began to fall away once they lost the faith of the people. Ironically, the strength of the tyrant was found to be in the tyrannized themselves, their belief and reverence. Let these erode, the power erodes.

So it is within. The quiet woman could be freed as soon as she lost her loyalty to the inner ruler, and she could do this by finding a new loyalty. Hence the importance of my attitude. I had to gain her trust: not her obedience, which would be a fresh tyranny, but her trust, something freely given, perhaps her first free act and tested bit by bit to the point of self-possession.

But how was I to be with her? I remember a story a friend tells of a mother watching her child paint. The child says, "Don't look at me that way." "What way?" "As if you were proud of me." The pride in the mother's glance falls on the child like an act of possession: how can she be free to do what she wishes? Maybe she hates painting; in any case she would not want to have to paint. My trustworthiness, too, must be established through successive acts of liberation, as much from me as from the inner tyrant.

My profession is often distrusted for imposing names and treatments and restraints on patients; I knew these had been applied to her as well. A psychologist and herself a student of the literature, she could be skeptical, but she was especially bitter because all these efforts had only increased her desire to die. I saw no need to defend the profession or my own efforts by learned technical discussion. My idea was not to impose more on someone I saw as already overpowered. I wanted to carry lightly whatever I thought I knew, perhaps thereby modeling my hope for her.

Imagery

She had undergone a long course of psychotherapy in which many interpretations and formulations were given, some of them, she thought, clever, even illuminating, but most of all depressing (there seemed so much wrong). For all the emphasis on free association, she never felt that this thinking was her own, any more than her own thoughts felt that way. She had also been pressed to doubt her parents' good will and competence. This was not as comfortable as blaming herself, which in fact most of the interpretations encouraged.

I decided there was a great deal I should not do. If the problem lay in the allegiance of her mind, I should secure this only if it were given freely. I wanted to deal with her mind in the same way I like to deal with my own, as an ally that works best when it it is let alone. So I set myself to avoiding the innumerable traps we put out for the capture of others. My own traps were typically bait for drawing conclusions, posing questions or enticements to reveal, the results of which might give me that precious sense of knowing who the patient really is, to counter the troubling confusion that any honest study of human nature always meets. I had to mind my own business, lest the compelling need to dispel suspense and identify the enemy make her a prisoner of my ideas.

I also wanted to avoid the traps she put out. Perhaps she hoped to discourage me or at least test the sincerity of my interest. She might want to discourage my interest because she didn't feel worthy of it or was afraid she would disappoint it. She might not feel able to bear one more falling away. I knew I couldn't meet every test of my genuineness or intensity or perseverance; that would not even be wise. If I fed such expectations, there could only be disappointment for her later in actual life. No, I would have to be honest, feel and persist within the easy reach of my capacities, or I would teach her wrong. The immediate fear I had was different: she might discourage me, get me to agree that she was distant, fragile, hopeless, and we should go our separate ways.

I wanted to say: I know you're discouraged, I know you think I'll fail, I know you believe my purposes will override yours—but perhaps not. The difficulty is that such words will successively cancel each other out, may be only half heard and add to her confusion. Again, the need of a gesture, the language of the body we learn to read before a book is opened. It must express what I felt, and be legible even with all the complexities of my attitude.

I think I smiled a little. I felt my body elaborate sentiments we both could read from it: my confidence, a belief in her, the desire not to intrude, a hope she would be comfortable here, a wish to take our time. Perhaps the last was strongest. I would think of something to tell the insurance company while the hours passed—time, I needed time. Also I didn't want us to meet very often, maybe once a week: this might send the right signal, that nothing will happen fast. I didn't want it to happen fast, in case the flower be forced, her own direction missed.

So I told her stories of my own life, what the children were doing, what I worried about. I hoped she wouldn't have to talk, to be captive to my expectations for her. And the more she knew about me, the easier it would be to decide whether I should be trusted. How else could she decide? Especially, I thought, she should know what I think is worst about me—my temper, my importunateness, a tendency to be arrogant, fussy, and secretly demanding—so that when these qualities swam into view she wouldn't be surprised and we could become allies against them. And I wanted her own limitations to be seen as inevitably human, no worse than mine, that we were together in this business of putting up with each other. I remembered, from the unlikely James Russell Lowell: "Whatever you may be sure of, be sure of this: That you are dreadfully like other people." It wouldn't be fair to let the so-called mentally ill carry the full burden of human nature.

The apparent thinness of her spirit, the impression she gave of being distant or barely present, was not the way it always felt to her. Taken up into the purposes and regulations of her internal ruler, she felt substantiated whenever she satisfied those rules; she gained protection. It was not only protection against the protector, or the pains of dereliction, but against the world at large. Such may be the most obscure part of these curious alliances.

The internal ruler appears to have external power because the tyrant is experienced as knowing the world, even controlling the world, as children see their parents. Accidental happenings can then appear to be punishments for fancied derelictions. The pervasive appeal of superstitions, of forces you can offset by a rabbit's foot or knocking on wood, springs from the same conviction of an inner order. In the mild form of a voice of conscience, we all receive the promptings that give both the private and the public sense of being right or wrong. Put differently, these standards are not simply guides to right thought and action for ourselves alone, but the very means by which we establish our place in the world. The passionate convictions common to religious beliefs have the same source. People fight so hard for their gods because they believe the gods protect them and, sadly, eagerly send them out against other gods. In this measure, most of us are prisoners.

A colleague once told me about a young man, seemingly miraculous in his grasp of the real world, who came to her because, she thought, he needed an established figure to tell him how to act. He had come a long social and economic distance from his family and perhaps for that reason felt uncertain of the standards to which he should conform. When he found that the therapist wouldn't tell him what to do, he pleaded, cajoled, insisted. It was remarkable because he knew his way around the world superbly, had a wonderful wife, a glistening career, good friends. But, afraid that his ambition and competitiveness would be exposed, he always expected to be humiliated even under safe conditions. We concluded that his parents' modest, homey virtues were still uppermost. Like the quiet woman, he needed to find his own way. So the therapist and the young man sat around together, he in search of a new god, she trying not to become one.

The successful patient was only too ready to switch his allegiance; the quiet patient was fearful. My colleague's successful life offered a tempting point for new rulership; any authoritativeness at all offered a tempting point for my patient. The colleague was afraid of disturbing the sound basis her patient had built; I was afraid that mine could not establish herself at all. In both cases the crisis came in a conflict of allegiances.

The successful man was the first to become discouraged. He decided to endure his shame and stop treatment since, he said, he was now ashamed of the treatment, which took forever and branded him as sick. If he had to decide between losing his humiliation and keeping his success, he would rather keep the success. Note that this was not a choice between the old, humble god and a new worldly one, since he was to continue with both shame and success. The outcome left him where he began.

My colleague and I had our treatment god, of course. Peace and harmony, you might guess, compromise and negotiation. No, something more ambitious—an escape from both the parents' and the world's dictation into the patients' own. This was my colleague's ideal all along, and her patient firmly resisted it. So what fresh power could she have at this apparently final moment?

It was simply that he did not want to leave her. He kept postponing his departure or promising to come back. We thought he did this because he couldn't take her with him; there was no space in his crowded pantheon. We also wondered if there were an ideal of both modesty and success that had been pitted against each other in his mental life. For the successful man to take a new ideal away with him, that ideal had to be as tall and definite as those ancient statues of the gods.

The attitude my colleague finally took expressed the feeling his conflict gave her, the struggle between ambition and modesty. Actually he could have them both, so her attitude said: "Your dream should be wild and wonderful, but so should your modesty, your awareness of danger and chance and envy, the sense that even the greatest goals land in your lap because you are as much the vessel of opportunity as its creator. You can enjoy it, love it, but offer up thanks. It's not a matter of unresolved sibling rivalry, life against death, conflicts between parent and child or between temperament and fit, none of the innumerable instances of contention that experience meets from its very start. All contribute to and render memorable what is in fact a given: that the resolution of life's struggles is painful and calls up the most creative energy we have." Surely a forlorn hope, that an attitude should say so much.

I don't think my colleague smiled. More likely she looked concerned, that the patient would give up the wise struggle between ambition and modesty he had begun. She would have liked something as unmistakable as a thunderclap to open the way. She had almost resolved to make a speech, eloquent and moving, when he did something that gave her an opening. His glance grew sparkling—he seemed to radiate energy—and he made a gesture she could almost feel on her skin. He was coming on to her! Words, words, no more words. The therapist told me she felt excited; it took some effort to stay calm and professional. Then she relaxed. I suppose it was because she had been given the opportunity she needed, to show him just what she meant. She said she admired him immensely and could even imagine the wonderful time they might have together. But that was not what she could best do for him. She could help him take his passion and turn it toward ideals that were neither modest nor competitive, neither self-effacing nor self-glorifying.

Well, I thought, I would like to do that for the quiet woman. Nothing so rapid or erotic, but still it would have much in common with what my colleague did in finding a new allegiance that could give space to both herself and others.

Selfishness was what my patient's ruler would not allow. She came to the problem of modesty and ambition from a point opposite to that of the young man. He had little room for others, she had no room for herself. They shared the all-or-nothing quality common to partly unconscious ideas. His conquests were global in fantasy, while her unselfishness had to stay complete. How to oppose those forces?

Since we all live in a world of inner and outer forces we can seldom control and often not recognize, the problem is easy to identify with. It only requires asking: Is what I do what I choose? How free am I to choose differently? The bravest, most ambitious spirit strikes against the rules of inner life, which are no less compelling than those of the culture. We could hardly walk if we tried to order the steps our feet take, yet ordinary dictation reaches far deeper than that, into the way we think. Even the freest effort of the most original spirit is mostly what we have heard, accepted, and believed. Still we stand up, prattle on, as I do here, dreaming we are not echoes or mimics.

The new emerges gradually, almost unnoticed. Einstein, struggling with his hesitations about Newtonian space, said he experienced physical movements, gestures of correction he found himself taking toward the prevailing views. It required two decades to transform those first protesting movements into the way we see the world. So what chance did I have?

I had the same chance he did, but with her protesting movements. She suffered, and part of her wanted to be free. Most of all I had the advantage of an enemy no longer accepted so completely in the world at large, this ruler, she said in retrospect, that controlled every move. It is said that the Roman mother did not decide when to have dinner; the hearth god knew and dictated. This power recedes. I remarked earlier that the greatest ally psychotherapy has gained in my time of work is the women's movement, which gives ideas and resources to offset sexism. The work of psychological healing rests on the resources of the emerging culture. When I set myself to free her, to be a new object of allegiance, I was not speaking for myself alone. Recall Freud, faced with the suppression of sexual thoughts, or Sullivan, taking on the power of social forces claiming everyone as their own. I had allies and needed only to represent them.

So we too sat around together. A stranger looking on would wonder what we were doing. Not much was said; there were no revelations, unless the growing safety she felt can be called that. Later she said it was a revelation to her, the comfort she had in the presence of someone who saw behind the public mask into her constriction and discomfort. I believe it was the new safety that set the stage for the conflict of allegiances. She became more secure going about her work, relatively free of concern that others think her different. At the same time, she thought more and more of death: she no longer wished to live enslaved, but the only way out of slavery seemed death, so formidable was the power controlling her. I thought of the revolutionary motto, liberty or death, here in the inner theater of one person's lifetime. I also believed this was not a stage play, that in fact she might die, that the choice was a real one because the slavery was both real and intolerable.

I was not entirely responsible for these realigned attitudes. She said she had always wanted to die. Yet I heightened her awareness of a life apart from slavery and thereby heightened her desire to die. Since I cared about her and was for all public purposes taking care of her, I was responsible.

Part of me wanted to talk her into life, to speak of Emerson's blowing clover and falling rain as if she could forget the deserts and the droughts. But all the while I tried to remember: make successive acts of liberation, not moving speeches or penetrating insights. Some of these acts had involved taking my time;

now she could take hers. Freedom would mean weighing and considering; she might want to round up the usual suspects, genes, parents, society, instincts, at whose door we put blame for the inner tyrants. But any pressure to decide must be a new rulership. I should treasure her indecision, clear a space around it. The fact that she felt uncertain was strong evidence of a waning allegiance.

My initial, arrested movement was only a little changed because it had been by my avoiding the expected that she could come to trust me. This is not quite right, for in surviving the silence and the fear, the possibility of death and all the opportunities for discouragement, I had been gaining confidence, in both of us, and this gave my posture a slight forwardness, even eagerness. Such was the bodily signature of my believing in her, which, although I didn't know it yet, was proceeding inch by inch with her growing belief in me. After she told me of no longer wanting to die, she also said she had come to trust me. Then I thought we might have won, that her allegiance was changed.

I faced a new temptation—to rejoice, to think we had made it. I could be forgiven relief, even if it was an uncertain relief, but it was important not to pretend that a world relatively free of tyranny is a much easier world. I believed she was entering the state of common humanity, swinging between freedom and authority, fearing freedom and bristling against authority. Freud said that the goal of treatment is to replace neurotic suffering with normal human misery. She was surprised; she thought life would be easier. The forces let loose had been better contained, tightly contained, before. Now she met them in the open air, to decide which ones to make her own.

She tried to be brave about the new dilemmas; she felt her allegiance to me meant that she should not complain. So I complained for her. She could begin to know liberty in her new alliance, test out for herself what price I might secretly have put on the work we did. Could I really let her go, now that she had what she needed from me? And could she go openly, undeterred by the claim she might make that she was as free as I was?

Possession

5 ~ Whose Am I?

At a christening many years ago, a child dropped her rattle. Without breaking his ecclesiastical rhythms the minister reached down, picked up the rattle, and handed it back to the child: "This belongs to you, Emily, but you do not belong to them," pointing at my wife and me. "You belong to God." Once again a third party, a minister this time, had entered the dialogue between the generations, speaking about possession and belonging. Perhaps I was ready to hear him because I had begun to learn the same lesson ten years before, when I had to share "my" older children with a stepfather. But what is the lesson? Most of us like to belong; we want to be attached to one another, to be part of a group or family. But no one wants to be property.

Sending the children off to camp we put names on their clothing, unnecessary in the smaller mixing bowls of home and family. We had already put our names on the children. The first names were "theirs"; the last names were useful only when they went off to school to show where they belonged. Most of the female children would lose their last names when they married, as slaves did if they changed plantations. A few innovative souls keep or combine their names when they make new families.

"Whose am I?" the young woman might have asked walking through my door. She could have said it plaintively, if she'd felt entitled to complain, because everywhere she went she met a curious indifference. I say curious because she was pleasant and very helpful. Yet seldom was anything made of her. Once I watched an intensely awkward person I knew enter a crowded room. She would find a group; the group would dissolve; then another. She was a solvent of togetherness: the smallest touch and others left. The young woman was not like that.

The resentment at being possessed is matched by the terror of being dispossessed. It is common to be psychologically evicted as decisively as if one's furniture were put out on the street. Think of foundlings, until they are found, or adoptees waiting to be adopted: who will have them? Yesterday I read of an adopted child who was sent back, the way defective appliances are returned, because of bad behavior. Many are the rich peoples' children fearful of being "disowned": possession, as usual, comes at a price.

Adopted people discover they have two sets of names. The birth certificate gives them one, the adoptive family another. Sometimes they discover a third, if the birth parents eventually thought of marrying. There is often shame in the first, a holding to the second, and a wish for the third: there I was, here I am, there I might have been. The young woman had only one set of names, but she prayed she could have another and be somewhere she felt wanted. As long as she could recall, she had wanted to be adopted, to have someone who would make her their own.

The names we are given attach us to events we are largely powerless to control, miserable events in the patient's case, often happy and enviable ones for others. The same thing happens when the psychiatrist calls someone schizophrenic; he or she is forever part of other lives pitiable and sequestered. It is a hard part to shake off, especially if the doctor is famous or convincing; after all, he is an expert in such matters, an umpire of the soul. Many live in an opposite world, waiting for banquets given in their honor. These names, ignominious or praising, comprise the influences we receive. It is an order of events with the force of the actual. Sometimes, as with the young woman, this order of events is intolerable and must be recast. That requires a power and persistence equal to the original events themselves. Then we discover people in both their pasts and our present because in the present we are drawn to name the patient by the same old names. The person does not arrive fresh and unknown; the old names stick. We need to break free, instituting a new order of events.

This I wanted to do. But the renaming, this repossessing, asked from me an energy and imagination from which I often flee. The hardest part was the most obvious, imagining her actual experience. It was not my failure of will or even of love. She was easy to love. Her energy and interest, her plain and unflagging devotion to others, her critical intelligence and perspective, all these were remarkable. I knew the words for her experience, but I couldn't imagine it.

The story is the story of a shipwreck. The lucky sail out into life, hopeful, equipped with examples, allies, the inner sails of this mentor or that, to brave the various tempests, visit the not so magic isles, and return home again with cargos of gifts and experience. Even Tennyson's lucky sound a melancholy note:

> And the stately ships go on
> To their haven under the hill;
> But O for the touch of a vanished hand,
> And the sound of a voice that is still!

But there are stories to tell and, best of all, listeners willing to hear. What if the stories turn every listener away, get one branded terrible or mad? What is there then?

Two years after her birth, the father died. Mother and child were then driven out of the in-laws' home, never to see them again. The mother left the child with grandparents and went to work in a distant city. The grandfather was a patriarch eager to protect and guide the child; he was married to the woman the patient loved most. Much of the time before college she spent with the mother's envied sister and her husband. The mother came and went, quarreling with this sister. The one topic mother and aunt could agree on was the patient's behavior, which was surely within the healthy range. Contemplation of the smallest disobedience would produce peace for a while, mother inwardly blaming the aunt, the aunt sure the child was like her mother. In order to produce these peaceful times the patient learned to caricature her faults, throw them up before the sisters' eyes. Later when she was criticized, she would do the same to bosses and colleagues, mocking herself. All through the time with the aunt and uncle she hoped they would adopt her, while they never knew whether the mother would return and take the child away.

Contrast this simple outline with the patient's experience. She had no memory of her father. He had been eliminated as completely as a disgraced revolutionary from the Soviet encyclopedia. The main thing the mother and grandfather did not dispute was this elimination. The patient's father and his family were never mentioned; the merest inquiry was a crime, and no message appeared from the forbidden other side. Here was a chilling lesson in the possibilities of nonbeing. Many years later she met the physician who had held the father when he died. She felt afraid to inquire: would there be fresh news to demoralize her?

Could she mourn him? In any settled community the great bulk of human losses are incomplete. Oh yes, we say, father died, but look, he is still everywhere. Friends mention him, the house he lived in and the surrounding mementoes of his existence crowd the living out. And our minds are full of him. The mention of his name releases a stream of images and associations that may give him dimensions larger than life. In fact, as we grow older our minds fill up with such remembrances, so that the past presses against a diminishing future. For the happy ones, death is little more than a sleep closing down this inner theater. Mourning is remembering. How could she mourn someone she never knew?

There was an irony in the forgetfulness, the historical elimination her family asked of my patient. It did not eliminate the little of his existence that she knew. Nor did it stop the widening wonderment of all she did not know. It was characteristic of this realistic person that the empty space and time about him did not fill up with fantasies of who he was and what he'd done. She collected every scrap of information, but the empty spaces remained. The irony was that forgetfulness appeared elsewhere in her life. It may have been a coincidence that she forgot dates, objects, and everyday events, to the great annoyance of her family. Or perhaps she was showing them how really forgetful she could become, which forgetting her father, since he went unmentioned, would never have done.

Just as I did not at first understand how literally the father had disappeared, so I did not grasp the one vividly experienced way he endured. The patient became a repository for the father's alleged badness, and sometimes of the mother's too. The patient was a kind of walking, talking testament to both their marred existences. The grandfather would say, "Don't be like your mother" or "What will become of you, with such beginnings?" With what felt to her like good intentions, the family marked her down as in grave danger, as teetering on the edge of an evil and a doom that her mother's visits embodied, an angry eccentric presence and absence that were irresistibly hers. In any catalogue of the circles of hell, this must have a supremely awful place: guilt by association, on the brink of great danger, treading an endless, difficult line, but also helped and warned so that the chance of being saved contributes to the endlessness. Nietzsche remarked that it was only by the thought of suicide that he got through many a dark night. I don't believe any such relief was open to her.

I am telling you how she existed for me. It is only through me that she exists for you, so you are in danger of inadvertently learning more about me than about her. But she suffered even more from my being the mirror of her being. She claimed she had been dead before we went to work, or at least asleep, so that awakening partly took on the form I could perceive and reflect back to her. I have said already that, in many instances, I plainly misunderstood, and in those instances she could detect the mistake and correct it. There must have been many other less obvious, therefore more insidious, distortions in my imperfect mirror.

She had always seemed to me a notably unpossessive person. She not only forgot and mislaid things, but did very little active seizing or collecting of them. Twice at deathbeds she had refused to accept beloved rings from significant people. I put this down to what I thought was her self-abnegation, her wanting little or nothing for herself. This was wrong: I was really turning her into the opposite of myself, a possessive person. In fact, self-abnegation was not the reason she refused the rings. It was the old story of her mother's desertion. Her mother had said, "I am leaving, what do you want?" "I want to come with you," she replied. That the mother never granted, but went on asking, "What do you want?" and offering candy, clothes, whatever. Because the daughter wanted only to go with her, she appeared selfless or ungrateful. It was this way with the rings. She didn't want to take them because she didn't want to acknowledge that these valued people were dying; in comparison with their continued, giving presences, any physical object lost all meaning. This is the way it often turns out to be with the seemingly unpossessive. They value objects for their human values; they love things when they are the repositories of people. They put me to shame.

The same example corrected a second misunderstanding. In seeking to understand her I often thought I was describing a pattern of nonexistence, the hell of nonexistence. There is a sense in which this was true. Yet the vitality and spirit she radiated suggested something else. I don't think these were mere animal spirits, however great her constitutional vitality. The world for her was full of spirits, or should I say spirit: opportunities to do good, possible friendships, contrasts between a living person and a dead metal. Of course these vital spirits often had the coloring of evil spirits, the various dangers, threats, and oppressions that crowded in on her. What was perhaps most extraordinary was the way she kept her feet in this spirit-filled world, not diminished to the point of destruction, as seems true of many psychotic persons, or plunged into a manic pursuit of fanciful images.

It is significant that this vital world survived all the numerous demands that she fake it. First she had to forget father and mother. The grandfather's most persistent command was for a low profile, that she not offend (like the mother) in order to avoid further disgrace to the family and any deviation from the traditional woman's role: assertions were "presumptuous." The mother's ideal of moral teaching restricted itself to a single demand, that she keep her underwear especially clean lest any hint of unmothering be conveyed. The aunt and uncle wanted her to pretend to be their child but never legitimized that state. A relative early suggested that the child's whole life would be improved if her diction improved. When I first met her, the current boss seemed chiefly interested in upgrading her clothing and that same diction. Yet the patient followed many of these commands while never losing her perception of the realities they were meant to disguise.

This lively person at first seemed to me an imposter of positive thinking; but unlike many imposters she fooled the world at the world's request. I thought, people said to her, "We know what we have done to you, but hide it, hide it"—and she had complied. Later I came to see that the world did not acknowledge this. Nor was she an imposter. People with meager or degraded existences often invent new ones, and the bravest are able to do more than fantasize: who can blame them? Now and then she thought of pretending to be married or having a different father or mother, but she had little taste for lies. And what she could not face about her existence no one else could have faced either. She only blunted her feelings. There lay in the basement of her mind a sinister rumble of what proved to be discontented thoughts; she always had to fight her way free of them. When they became more fully articulated, as simple disgruntlement, she was terrified. Surely I must be disgusted with her, surely I wanted only the sunny smile and pleased enthusiasm both natural to her and the safest ticket out of orphan land. Appreciate, appreciate, her experience cried out to her; otherwise they will be merciless. This is the etiquette of outsiders: be polite even to the awful.

I remembered that mood. It had occurred to me first in my own family, where my father's disgruntlement and my mother's low spirits threw a burden of support and encouragement on my sister and me. It occurred still more imperiously in the army and later during my early career at Harvard. The men I worked for valued enthusiasm—they may not have been too sure of themselves. Further, the wise student of institutions learns to look the other way, to take little note of the boss's weaknesses, certainly to identify with purposes perhaps at variance with his own. Many times I remember fearing the chief's displeasure when the real displeasure was mine. Eager for security, hopeful of promotion, afraid of poverty, most of us compromise. My patient had far more compelling reasons for loyalty than I ever did, so understanding that aspect of her plight came easy.

What does a child do when a mother is so strange? The child turns to its father or a sibling. She had neither. As a result, the mother sat in the middle of her mental life, shouldering to one side any image of happy sociability. The patient had to work the periphery of experience, taking up a position just outside. She had to make little of herself, lest the strangeness be noted.

She could not disown this creature she needed, a creature who in any case reappeared unbidden. There were few memories she could bring to human meeting. It often seemed to me that the mother, herself deeply disappointed, was schooling the child in every trick of fate. The mother might have said: I want her to know and experience whatever sad turn of events can occur. There were many instances, but one had the simplicity of a paradigm. The mother failed to send birthday cards. The patient carefully avoided complaining. The mother attacked her for not complaining: didn't she care about cards from her mother? The mother was saying that there's no place on this planet for contentment.

Still the patient always cared for her mother, in life, in sickness, and in death. As is not uncommon, a stroke improved the mother's disposition so that the last years were relatively free of venom. And the young woman bought the tombstone, held the service, buried her. Perhaps to the end and after, she was trying to calm that critical, independent spirit, give it rest so that she could rest too. It is hard to settle with parents.

Many times she gave me books and articles to illuminate her experiences. She said Charlotte Brontë knew aspects of her life. Tony Tanner's introduction to the starkest of novels, *Villette*, speaks of Lucy Snowe's effort "to constitute herself in a society largely indifferent to her needs." "Lucy is everywhere not-at-home," unbonded. For a while she does find solace in a small room, "somehow like a cave in the sea," but this is confining, like an asylum in which one hides but cannot develop. My patient occasionally broke out of her frightened acquiescence to the estranging modes of her existence, feeling an anger that disoriented her. She would then check carefully to be sure our bond was still there. The job she had, under a so that the world can be regularized, steadied, dehumanized, in the service of manners and order.

Lucy Snowe often dealt with this world by becoming part of the furniture, another thing. My patient dealt with it by becoming a servant. Indeed, she and I shared a central passion for the development of others. This arises from pain in the presence of incomplete existences, the capacity to have one's self penetrated and hurt by the felt tragedy of such an existence. Both Lucy and the patient were frequently surprised by the indifference most people show toward tragedy. It is true that many record it, take its impression, even observe it accurately, but at a distance where the observer is more like a spy than a participant. Tanner invokes Hawthorne and James as writers troubled by the moral ambiguity of observing rather than acting. It is no accident that the book you are reading begins with the words of a novelist who made his participation in just such a society the basis of a book of great moral force, perhaps of therapeutic power too. But Proust could turn both the experience and the creation into gratitude and reward.

I believe the need to fill up the lack in her existence propelled her, forced her, to search that meager existence for any bit of sustenance, the occasional happy contact. Most often these were exchanges with children as yet unburdened by manners or power. Her pain, constantly elevated by the penetration of others' plights, was only briefly relieved, most of all because she *felt,* that is, she was much more conscious than many of what she lacked. In psychological work, especially with families and marriages, the dominant metaphor is often of war. Here it was drought or famine. Lucy Snowe often refers to cups or bowls, to a stone basin in a park "brimming with cool water." Naturally, in both cases, there are outbreaks; the work proceeds

man still more critical and demeaning than her mothe
her tightly. The boss confined the whole department by
tests of appearance and decorum, and rewarded those
social position and connections elevated his own. The rɪ
not one of machines, as was true of Lucy's villainous M
Beck, but that of fashion models, serene, almost faceless,
mannered. Perhaps the starkest contrast to Lucy and the ɪ
is another character in the novel, Ginevra, who is obsesse
clothes and ornaments. Indeed the word "thing" is us
Ginevra constantly and fills in for persons and places
strength of her selfishness appears extraordinary to Lucy
patient also marveled at such characters in her world, ch
them on, and often became an instrument of their purɪ
Gradually there arose a satirical note in this cheering on
she wished to advertise the selfishness, mimic the wɪ
support of it, and expose the results.

It astonished me that the patient could preserve her iɪ
rity in a world so indifferent to her. In fact her inte
flourished because the artificiality of prevailing rules and
general acceptance left a wide berth for simple expressivɪ
and attention to others. Perhaps this was a reason for her ɡ
humor and generally high spirits: there was much useful ʋ
to be done. Nevertheless she was frequently undone, cryin
becoming "unduly" excited. This too stood in contras
everything cold and planned around her. It was as if
harbored all the feelings frozen or put aside by the others.
one could "duly" contain so much. Nor is the cold wɪ
Brontë described rare, or the similar world the patient lived
Think how often people are condemned for showing nervo
ness or even excitement. Whole social and diagnostic syste
are constructed to outlaw the most ordinary displays of feeliɪ

by fits and starts and then fresh suppressions. As Lucy says, "We shall and must break bounds at intervals, despite the terrible revenge that awaits our return." I see this revenge as springing from a partial identification with the oppressive forces, the very self-mortification, in my patient's case, that so placated her mother and aunt.

One result was sharp alternations of feeling, which deeply upset the patient; her whole world could turn upside down. Often I urged her to call me after we had met because I predicted something she had said would be not just regretted, but felt as destructive of what she held most dear. Yet my availability had a price. Her respect for me was reinforced at the cost of once again becoming an object of obedience. "We must be careful," I said, "that we see this as a matter of respect, not of servility." I must not see her, as Lucy is often seen, as a child in need of protection. It must not be a child that is protected but someone under seige, as we best see ourselves, alive and in danger. As a patient she could not be well protected either. Patienthood implies possession by one or other category of disease; in the psychological sphere, these are inherently problematic. Both Lucy and the young woman illustrate this. Lucy often saw her isolation and denigration in the medical, psychiatric terms of her day, which were phrenological. Ironically my patient, the least narcissistic of people, saw herself in that currently fashionable term. So rigorous was her argument for this point that it would have been easy to let her carry the day, as commonly happens in psychological diagnosis, the patient making the case, in both senses. As is true of most human attributes, it is possible to see any self-regard, however fleeting, in pathological terms, specifically as evidence of sick narcissism. On the other hand, scientific efforts call out for quantitation, which is absent here. The diagnosis was difficult to discourage because to be narcissistic was at least to belong to a popular group, perhaps the only one this neglected person could aspire to. Here at least she would belong.

Lucy's harrowing cry is still relevant: "The world can understand well enough the process of perishing for want of food: perhaps few persons can enter into or follow that of going mad from solitary confinement. They see the long-buried prisoner disinterred, a maniac or an idiot!—how his senses left him—how his nerves, first inflamed, underwent nameless agony, and then sunk to palsy—is a subject too intricate for examination, too abstract for popular comprehension . . . And long, long may the minds to whom such themes are no mystery . . . be few of number, and rare of encounter. Long may it be generally thought that physical privations alone merit compassion, and that the rest is a figment" (Penguin edition, p. 39).

Lucy Snowe, for whom read Charlotte Brontë, found her protection in writing books. Tanner says, "She can only be herself to the extent that she can speak herself." I wanted the patient to find her protection in conversation with me. She said she had, but it didn't seem so for a long time. And this was for a reason that crowned Freud's therapeutic system: the illness reappears in the treatment, which is a danger as much as an opportunity. Her "illness" reappeared as my failure to understand it; because of that failure, it stood in danger of being confirmed and deepened. Just as Brontë had to find the voice that produced *Villette,* so the patient and I had to find voices that would create a mutual understanding, in which she was not a child, an ill person, or someone perpetually misunderstood. Tanner argues that Brontë's difficulty in speaking was a result of a male-dominated society. This was certainly a factor in the patient's lot too—hers was a woman's profession, for example—but her oppressors were often women as well and, to a considerable extent, she was a minority of one. Brontë's difficulties do not seem to me solely those of women either; her world has been described as cold, mechanical, and materialistic, one in which women are not strangers.

The patient and I reconstructed her life. The products of reconstruction were supposed to be better parts of that life. Often they were the old parts. For example, the pride she could not take in herself she continued to take in others, including me. She continued to carry Freud's formula for mature development to its outer reaches: all her self-love flowed into others. I wanted to shout, "Reverse the golden rule, do unto yourself what you do unto others. Don't confirm what Marx and Nietzsche preached, that goodness is a request for exploitation." Only gradually did I see a subtle loosening of the old bonds. She became less protective of me, began to correct statements I made. And within her own mental life demands were not so automatic and obeyed. She began to converse with images of grandfather, grandmother, mother, and other significant figures. Dialogue had begun; free speech and the rights of independent assembly were gathering strength inside; she was not so identified with the old authorities. Still later the tone of her inner agencies changed. They lost some of that corrective, negative, commanding air: they became more like the imaginary companions of a lonely childhood, supportive and consoling.

More and more I asked myself what seemed the burning social question of her life: why are some people treated so badly? I couldn't fall back on the hints of an answer the sociology of childhood has suggested, that some children fail to learn the social language, gestures, and perceptions of their peers, and therefore blunder over and over again into outcast states. She had good friends in childhood; she actively and successfully sought them out. It was as if the world of her adulthood re-created her childhood experience of adults (she was most at home with children); the family at work became the family of origin. But this neat formula is not quite true either. After college she had a series of jobs caring for children, often very difficult children, and had been quickly and repeatedly recognized as gifted in this far beyond the ordinary. Parents, fellow teachers, and researchers rewarded her. The difficult time came later, in a famous hospital, under that clever and manipulative boss, where she languished unpromoted for ten years (if this busy and effective woman can ever be said to have languished).

I often tell eager young people leaving school and taking up their first jobs: beware, your eagerness and the boss's needs can build a prison stronger than Alcatraz. In our most successful institutions, leaders are often sought and found among those most gifted at enslaving the young. Thus are empires built and reputations enhanced. There is an old story of a young doctor returning from a much-sought interview with his famous chief. The apparently fortunate young man looked downcast, and a friend asked why. The young man said the interview had been successful, he was praised, in fact called a "man of promise." "Well, then, why are you sad?" the friend asked. "Because I know what that means. It means I'll promise to do the great man's work for him. This is one of life's gilded lemons." Rare it is for leaders to put the individual interests and futures of their charges first; commoner to possess and be possessed.

The famous hospital gave her countless opportunities for service; the atmosphere of energetic, skillful doctors and nurses partly offset her many humiliations; and there were always young people, medical students, new trainees, freshly hired colleagues, with whom she could identify and for whom she was a sure resource. She who asked too little for herself assisted many who were ready to ask too much. In any large organization, jobs abound that nobody wants. Finding able and willing hands is perhaps the leadership's top priority, preferably hands that will stay useful year after year and not pass their tasks from the once youngest to the now youngest. Too much praise, even any praise at all, may loosen the willing hold on the undesirable work; better to conspire with any diminished self-esteem. Above all the leader hopes—meanwhile consoling what conscience the leader has left with the thought that this person is fortunate to have any job at all—years will pass and the victim will grow too old to be desirable elsewhere, so that her final decades can be spent where she began. At the end there are goodbye parties, little ceremonies of self-forgiveness, in which sad speeches and only slightly brighter gifts oil the passage into oblivion.

Life has taught me that the decency of unflagging responsiveness occurs most often where our ideas of the conditions of healthy development make it least expected. It is the Cinderella story. I remember reading that story often to my children, sometimes when I was being taught the conditions of healthy development. But here was Cinderella: her mother dying at her birth, her father remarrying an unpleasant woman and then dying himself, and the stepsisters. Everything went wrong. Yet Cinderella was a dear, devoted, hard-working, attractive, forgiving woman. Reaction formation, you may say, sadness and hostility turned into an unnatural goodness or a blind search for love. I don't know about Cinderella, but I think I knew my patient. Her goodness rang true. It did not have the edge of rage or the manipulativeness of bribery. Nor was she of that happy lot who know from an early age their effect on people, happy if it is a happy effect. They come on in that steady, faintly beaming way that announces you will like and admire them, which you do. No, that wasn't the result she expected. Her goodness seemed goodness for its own sake.

She had experienced hostility, indifference, selfishness, most cuttingly from her mother, and she had set herself never to be like that. Her ideal was formed, as ideals so often are, in the burning fire of pain. But she had not thereby escaped an identification with her mother. She took toward every failure of her reaching the ideal much the same scathingly critical attitude her mother had taken toward her. What was most striking to me was that she did not project that fierce conscience on others; she did not distort, so far as I could tell, their attitudes toward her. In relatively unstructured contacts, as when she tried to free-associate on my couch with me out of sight, there was a disturbing fear that the other would be critical, even turn into her mother. But this was rare: she was slow to perceive hostility.

Much of the hostility she experienced, I believe, was real and a function of her foreignness. I do not here leave my theme of image and the real because she had been given an image, of foreignness, of the dispossessed. She was like the homeless, except that others acknowledged her homelessness only in their rejection. This had to be an excruciating state because even sympathetic people turned off any account she tried to give of her experience: it was too foreign. Her history was literally unspeakable. She was alone in regard to the most important parts of her experience, both for others and herself. Coming to life, in this case coming into her own country, meant battling the sources of both my resistance and hers: my thinking I understood when I didn't, or my not being able to understand and her fearing I would turn aside.

Sociability depends on the capacity to identify with one another; we belong. This is why images and conventions are so important. We take on the one—I wear the right clothes—and communicate by the other—I know what to say—in order to make the process of mutual identification possible. Friendship inhabits the precious territory between society and solitude: my friend and I can be alone together. And solitude itself is the necessary protection against the price paid for images and conventions.

Those with whom others do not identify are either consigned to oblivion or make up their own society in another tribe. Many wish to belong who cannot. Some are imposters manipulating the images and conventions of society with no settled identification. She was among those who do not manipulate, those on whom society can therefore practice self-assertion, the savagery forbidden within the tribe. The tribe could not identify with her. Her motives were either too obvious or too obscure; and everything she revealed about herself was an affront to the conventions that prevailed. The geniuses of orphanhood create new societies, whether a fresh religious sensibility, a comradeship of the adopted, the open alliance of once-secret drinkers, or the great movements of minorities and women. By this means each alien group belongs. What gave special poignancy to my patient's lot was its individuality: she was not adopted, not technically an orphan. There was no group of like others she could seek out or be known by.

Note what the group can do that no one can do alone. I have watched adopted people join groups searching for roots and birthparents. At one meeting I saw an adoptee I knew sitting between her birthmother and her adoptive mother. Immediately I felt sad for the adoptive parent, who had to see the extraordinary physical likeness of birthmother and child. I could imagine the adoptive parent's sorrow and estrangement, she who had reared the child, renamed it, perhaps confident that she possessed her, now evidently another's. Later I learned that the same adoptive parent came to see the birthmother as the completion of the adoptive mother's infertile existence; they could possess each other. First each had to confess a flaw in their relationship to the child. The birthmother felt she could not be forgiven for having surrendered the child. The adoptive mother felt their relationship was incomplete, not having borne the child. The two mothers needed each other, as they had much earlier. But now the need was confessed and completed as the images of guilty woman and barren person gave way to acceptance of incompleteness and each other. Putting back together what had been torn apart was to become part of one another. All three completed the empty spots in their existences by an identification with one another.

But how could my patient complete her existence? Can we ever learn to treat ourselves well without the example of being treated well? Even I who wanted this for her sometimes didn't respond. I asked for her sadness, disappointment, bitterness; hearing them I sometimes turned aside. Years after this began, a friend cast some light. He described studies that had been made of interviews with holocaust survivors. One observation came straight home to me. When the talk got to the horror of the survivors' experience, the interviewers wanted to escape. Sometimes this took the form of insisting that survivors could have escaped; more often, they had made mistakes, were somehow wrong or even evil; still more often, the escape effected was the interviewers' own. They simply could not attend.

Set yourself not to possess or abuse or escape another human being, and you see quickly the thin curtain separating our hope of civilization from the savage practices of slavery and cannibalism. Most loving couples begin their relationship with a stern resolution to honor and respect. And yet they have hardly left the church before the slowness of one or the haste of the other, the disappointment of one expectation or the unwanted fulfillment of another, reveals the snarling beast. Just as sternly I resolved to honor and respect my patient. Her virtues were a crown anyone would be proud to wear. Yet I turned aside.

I remember once telling a young physiotherapist—newly embarked on the treatment of my left hip—that the exercises she prescribed were not helping. Immediately she burst into tears. That I could handle. But then she sniffled them back, said it was her allergy and that I must have been doing the exercises wrong. She had to blame me. Much of what professional skill provides is not skill at all but perseverance. Most of the race casts a frightened glance from a car window past the scene of an accident, while medical students learn to turn toward the horrors of the flesh: blood, bones sticking through skin, vomit, even the facts of death become matters of professional interest. At its best, psychological training is also a great immunization; now the horror is panic, fury, the unbelievable, forbidden yearnings, including the yearning to die. Much that patients tell us is little more than a test of our courage. My patient showed an old hand how much he still had to learn. God knows it was harder on her than it was on me. I had the joy of knowing there was more to learn; the work had not grown routine and prescriptive.

I battled my enemies. Foremost was her habit of concession, which occupied the place of any right to want. I suspect that right receded when her strongest wish was denied, when her mother left her. It became like an unused and atrophying muscle that must be gently exercised. On the one hand, there was to be nothing of her own; on the other, she had learned to be on her own—so how could she use me? I had to offer, suggest, praise, and then bear her refusals, because for a time nothing good could stick to her, only the negative and critical. Meanwhile I must protect her against a remarkable fact. She was very real, she had no false self, she wore her heart on her sleeve, and few could resist a passing slap. She did the same thing to herself. She loved to talk with children, so she called herself childish when it was honor she merited. The entitled forget how the unentitled feel. Once she told me she had been afraid to mention her sadness at my vacations because that might intrude on and spoil those vacations. Hating was even harder because she felt so readily the other's point of view. She could even empathize with her mother's leaving. And she knew what it was to be hated. Early in life she had hated her mother and told her so. Then it began to cost too much. The slave who hates grinds himself to death, not the master; only with the prospect of liberation is hate useful. But she was afraid I would hate her for hating. I must love her hating, all of it.

More and more she seemed the opposite of many I have known, the psychologically dead who walk among us, their condition hardly noticed because they grunt and sometimes talk, the way hair and nails grow on bodies otherwise deceased.

The proud lawyer or the woman with the chestnut hair could have become hollow inside their stately or glamorous shells. I met a boyhood friend forty years later. He had been the star of our group, a sweet-spoken southern boy beloved by young and old. He had lived off a charm so strong that neither he nor the charmed could resist. Stretching behind him was a trail of suicides and broken hearts, broken homes and new conquests. You felt bewilderment echoing inside the emptiness, while the charm still clung to the quiet manly voice. Years ago, how we had envied him!

What she liked most was for me to tell her about myself and my family. So I did: what happened on holidays, the happiness and unhappiness, what the children said, and the grownups, my own history. She was an eager listener and a kind commentator. I was giving her what she had missed. And she gave me her eagerness, her great spirit, her wisdom, the details of an unusual life. We were filling each other in. She couldn't have children now. I did that. I couldn't understand children as she did. She let me know. Recall that we discover only fragments of people in their pasts. Much more comes forward now, in these reactions that can focus hopes and energies. On this ground, beyond possession, we take on new names and become parts of one another.

6 ～ A Possessor

Powerful people come into treatment more often than they once did because of marriage counseling and family therapy. In the old days it seemed there were two classes, victims and victimizers, one group sinned against, the other sinning, one taking responsibility and the other blaming. It is this way throughout medicine: the reckless driver or the pneumococcus, the cancer itself, does not seek treatment. It is the trauma victim, the patient struck by car or tumor, who comes for help. Yet the two often arrive together, as in infections and family work; now and then a blamer gets talked into psychotherapy.

He hadn't wanted to come. For months, in fact, he only pretended to come. It is remarkable to be in the presence of a lively and determined person who is so little there. It is like talking to a half-attentive person at a cocktail party who awaits someone else. I remember how I felt in my own first experience of treatment. I was afraid to seek help, so I became a candidate in a psychoanalytic institute, able to hide my needs behind a screen of education and professional advancement. I didn't want to look at myself.

He didn't want to look at me or himself. Not wanting to look at me was a good sign, of his reluctance to deceive or attack me. The need for self-protection was not that deep; he was more bewildered than contentious. I may have felt that I should tell my analyst something, if only not to give the game away. I suspect my patient felt that way too, waiting it out, until his wife (who had sent him) should decide he was all right.

To start with, he said he masturbated. He said it with astonishing reverence, not for the act itself but for a divine presence he seemed to conjure up to accept this offering. I felt like saying, "What do *you* think about doing it?"—to establish his not being alone in this awful act and perhaps to expose whatever exciting images he had. No doubt the most harmless sexual behavior in existence, masturbation excites extraordinary shame. I have known grown people to speak of it as if they were confessing murder or imprisonment. Once I asked the staff of a hospital service I ran what provisions there were for the patients' "solitary joys" (or some such phrase). The staff knew immediately what I meant and became quietly psychotic. A similar effect is achieved, I understand, by opening an umbrella in a group of swans. Naively I talked about the lengths that boys at camp were driven to and something I had once read about the Eskimos. The staff began to look at me as if Satan had arrived. I got out of there quickly and tried to look very respectable during my next several meetings.

He then said something about not pleasing his wife. Figuring that he might view me as the lady's hired gun, I said she might not always be so pleasing herself. He brightened visibly. There followed a great rush of talk that I tried not to hear in detail. He had an understandable need to justify himself in these circumstances, and I didn't think it wise to allow any unwitting response or gesture that close attention to arguments provokes; I didn't want to agree or disagree at this point. But I couldn't help hearing that the wife had lots of money and was paying for this very hour. Plainly he and I were in this together; in one sense we were both hired guns.

I wonder if any treatment can begin before the patient has been turned into a victim of something, if only of himself. The couple's therapist who had referred him spoke of the patient's demeaning nature, called him "sensitive and abusive." I didn't want to hear that either. I wanted to make up my own mind. Treatment beginning as a cabal of professionals to correct some poor soul's sickness or neurosis inevitably becomes adversarial. The patient quite justly feels that plans are afoot to which he has little access; he can't even locate his accuser. Moreover, the image of an unpleasant person sticks in the therapist's mind.

The idea that people are more or less toxic jumbles of impulses, defenses, punitive consciences, or some disease state gives the doctor a lot to do. The good patient and the busy doctor can look on the toxic jumble with a confident eye to improvement. I remember a plumber's inspection of the first house I owned. He went down to the cellar, looked up at the pipes, gravely tapped a few, and then shook his head. That was many years ago. I was poorer than I am now and younger in the ways of the world. With no money to replace those diseased pipes, I lived with them for seven years and, I was later told, could have lived with them another seven. You never would have guessed that from the solemn plumber.

Now I was the solemn plumber, with a jumble on my hands. There were two young children, much talk of divorce, three stepchildren from previous marriages, and the wife's powerful, angry father. Two months into the treatment I learned from the patient that he was having an affair. He thought he had successfully concealed this from the family. Earlier I had heard from the other therapist that the patient was an unemployed musician.

I told him I was distressed to hear about the affair; the problem was not so much the affair itself as his having told me. There was already too much stacked against him—he could be ridden out of town on a rail. I hoped he would not get it into his head to tell anyone else. I mumbled something about the powerful father's possibly having spies and the dangers of optimism and innocence. He said he had told me only because he was desperate. He didn't know whether he should leave his wife, and there was no one else to talk to.

He didn't look desperate. There was a quiet charm and something superior about him, even patronizing. I felt a little privileged just to have him in the room. But it was a long time before I appreciated the extent of his power. This was partly because he didn't appreciate it either. He always felt on the edge, even in his new affair.

He also had a melancholy air. It was not distasteful; he obviously felt at home with it. I came to suspect that if brain chemists could map his brain they would find many receptors for bittersweet experience. It was a mood he gravitated to, could not shake off. There had been much to accustom him to it early in life. It was also one of the means by which he possessed his wife, who found it moving. She had devoted herself earnestly to cheering him up. It was not that way with the new woman. After a brief and wonderfully exciting month, she had turned indifferent. This was a source of great bewilderment. Just as his melancholy excited the wife, so the new woman's indifference motivated him. He tried harder and harder to reignite her. In fact each of the possessed ones was rewarding the possessor's worst behavior. He was not so deeply trapped as the wife because his melancholy turned the new woman off; escape was possible.

I didn't know that yet, so I contemplated this busy picture with some melancholy of my own. The possessor was himself possessed. It reminded me of my experience of tennis. Many tennis players think they exist in a little tennis world of their own, in which success or failure turns on their sneakers or the racket or their mood of the day. In reality there are innumerable levels of ability. If you venture one step up or down, your defeat or victory is assured. I believe it is this way in the human world at large. People's power is similarly graded, and woe to the one who steps too high. The happiest marriages, in my experience, are between equal players, which is true of tennis matches as well.

I had come to one firm conclusion for this patient: nothing should change quickly. If he returned home now, he would be leaving the most exciting experience of his life. If his wife threw him out, he might discover that the new family was even less manageable than the old. Perhaps the wife didn't yet want to lose him. Where did that leave us?

Powerful people used to come into treatment mostly because they needed a cover, just as people in prison sometimes become psychotic in order to move out of dangerous places into safer hospitals. In practice it is very difficult to tell the feigned illness from the real one. The reluctant patient became an enthusiastic one as soon as he realized that the image or role of patient was a useful cover. The wife would give him time while he "worked on his problems." The father-in-law had been thrown a bone. Even the new woman responded; she modified her behavior, knowing it was being reported to someone else.

I was sitting pretty. If I could turn the holding pattern into a holding environment, if we could take the cover of "patient" to whatever this bewildered man needed to make a life, I could surpass what I have too often been for powerful people, a brief sojourn between temporary setbacks and new conquests. But I was sitting pretty for an unpretty reason. The man was nearly bankrupt. He no longer believed in his power to make the world he wanted. He had failed as a musician, in fact been humiliated. His second marriage was close to gone. The new woman had already disappointed him. And there were the children.

Everyone knows that concern for children has kept many a marriage going. The reason is not only concern for the children but the children's concern. As a rule families are little cauldrons of political action. Freud demonstrated this for oedipal issues, and it is true for many others. Children are seldom fans of divorce. I believe this man's son began a quiet act of diplomacy between his father and mother that helped to prevent an immediate break. He knew he was the apple of his father's eye, and he became more attentive to the mother. The patient's disapproval of his wife thus struck against the son's approval. To keep the son's affection he had to make peace with the wife.

This somewhat stabilized the busy scene. But it would be a curious treatment that hinged on the bankruptcy of the patient. He came into treatment because he was forced to. He remained because it was a useful cover. Once he would have said that success meant repossession of the wife and his old image of the romantic musician. Now he didn't know what success meant. At times it felt like staying alive.

There began a long period in which he revealed remarkable power. For most of this time it was power born in desperation: he had to please the difficult woman, preserve his son's loyalty, not offend the wife, and avoid the father-in-law. He also began to rethink his musical career. His life reminded me of those old Marx Brothers films in which six plots are hatched simultaneously, every one chaotic. He also had to play all the brothers.

I recalled a lesson of my own life. It isn't always good to get what you want; perhaps you don't know what you want; perhaps what you want isn't good for you. I remember how hard I worked to preserve my own first marriage and how wise now I think my first wife's decision was to end it. She saw more deeply than I did into our difficulties. She didn't agree that I knew what was good for me or us. Of course it would be as unwise to encourage therapists to tell patients what they should want as to assume that anyone else knows. It happens enough anyway. The best we have to offer is a safe place in which to review possibilities, explore, let a judgment form.

I had the advantage of a patient so careful, quick-witted, and even prudent as to keep all those Marx Brothers plots in order. There was a particularly critical period when the father-in-law stirred. The patient needed money, the wife was suspicious, the amounts called for were large. Twice before the rich man had helped his son-in-law, in the failed musical career. Now the patient planned to finish his conservatory training, toward the goal of teaching music himself. This had the advantage of being respectable, public, perhaps within reach. It had the disadvantage of being expensive and prolonged, implying a commitment to the son-in-law which neither his past performance nor future prospects, as professor of music or continued son-in-law, made reassuring. So the patient had to persuade him. He approached the father-in-law with what seemed the perfect mixture of confidence and humility, of grave concern and lightness of heart. Humility and lightness were as necessary as confidence and concern because he knew the rich man detested being pressured, especially by someone he detested anyway. He got his money, for four years. I felt like sending him to the Middle East.

It was important that I not be neutral, certainly not moralistic toward an effort that would not appeal to everyone. I actually threw myself into it. Some would feel I was nourishing a psychopathic bent for someone already showing promise in that direction. Again, I didn't think it was my job to police him. There were enough others for that. I would not have felt the same way if he had planned to murder the rich man and steal his money.

But he was doing nothing really wrong. In fact he put much of the money to solid use, and I avoided a moral position more doubtful than his own. Much of so-called proper behavior is the lack of disguise that powerful people would like to impose on the disadvantaged, an openness of presentation they would never exercise themselves. Many professionals expect of patients and students levels of frankness and compliance that are light years from their own. These are ways of keeping control or possession. If I was not to collude in dangerous games, I had to support the musician, and support meant protecting his safety in such games. Sometimes professionals have a larger stake in propriety than they do in their patients, with the result that they appear like timid surgeons: fearful of cutting into a tumor, they let the patient die.

Having secured the money, he hurried off to the indifferent woman. Here the improprieties were greater still. Probably some of the father-in-law's money went to his daughter's rival. How could I countenance that? Diplomacy and tact are one thing, you say; theft and deception are another. Try rationalizing that! Perhaps I am a thief myself because I can, and the thieves and murderers I have known were all great rationalizers. An old friend once asked me to interview a man in prison who had killed another man while robbing his store. The imprisoned man had helped my friend start a halfway house for other prisoners being released without homes or communities of their own. He seemed to my friend an exemplary person, honorable, trustful, and effective. The hope was to get him paroled. Several times I went inside the great concrete walls, as imposing as pyramids, past the steel and iron doors, down the bare, brightly lighted corridors, more inhuman than even hospitals and airports, to see the upright, steady man. (I think often of that prison, an image of safety and justice shown over and over again to spawn more violence and crime.)

The imprisoned man told me he was the firstborn of many children, to alcoholic parents; early he had taken food from stores to feed the younger ones. He said he didn't know how the storeowner had died. The light was dim, shots were fired; he still felt it was a dream, never happened. There was no way I could tell if this was deception, self-deception, a part of his past but no longer part of his future, or some strange truth. I wish we had such ways of knowing. With the musician my job was simpler. I didn't have to find propriety or the truth. I had to make things turn out well.

Part of me has always identified with Franz Kafka. The castle and the court and the prison are mysteries that deceive even the people in charge. The possessors are again possessed. The other day I read a speech by the writer Vaclav Havel, who in a strange time found himself president of Czechoslovakia. He is greatly surprised and expects to lose his job any minute. A writer becoming president of a country is paradox enough, but he also identifies with Kafka. "The lower I am," he said, "the more proper my place seems; and the higher I am, the stronger my suspicion is that there has been some mistake." Havel is therefore ready to be relieved and will not be surprised when the police come. Oddly, George Washington had a similar thought. Amid all the pomp and adulation of his inaugural day he said to a companion that, except for one or two turns of chance, he might be going to his hanging. In a difficult time of my own, I coined a saying: the unexpected is the only thing that happens. It is a paradoxical source of tranquility to know that we live close to failure and death.

I wanted the patient to learn about and deal with the indifferent woman because he could not return home until he had. He was beginning to feel like Kafka himself, "alienated and ashamed," as Havel put it. This was because he was beginning to feel her power. Sexuality is a wonderfully rich field for the exercise of power; the chances offered to intrude, stimulate, frustrate make it a dangerous place for those less in possession of themselves. My patient had begun to worry about his potency. He was experiencing the wide and open avenue the body is into the self. Young people begin to learn this in the experience of self-consciousness. I watch my body for its reaching or disappointing an image I have of myself; I am at the mercy of my body; I reclothe it, repose it, and check again. When the patient placed his slightly aging body naked beside the attractive woman, her eyes, like the adolescents', connected his body to his soul. The verdict of those eyes traveled the open road to his psychological being and left him shattered or comforted. Of course all aging tries the intimacy of our relationship with our bodies, but when the self gives its possession of itself over to the keeping of the body, it serves a fickle master.

Or a fickle mistress. He was learning about another intimate relationship, between anger and lust. The would-be professor of music said he was surprised to note that "the best sex" had a savagery about it, just short of killing. In fact she had used that word to describe how wonderful he made her feel. Sexuality was then almost literally a conquest; she was for a moment possessed. So this period of their fighting had both their best moments and their worst. I never knew whether he would arrive exhilarated or depressed. What did become clear was his growing exhaustion.

He was still more depressed by the reappearance of her two former husbands. She seemed ready to drop him and pick up again with either or both of them. He who had never been a loyal man felt a sudden attachment to loyalty and recommended it to her. She reminded him where he was coming from, which he ruefully admitted. But his feelings were hurt and he nursed schemes of revenge. This struck me as perfectly natural results of her power and his helplessness. We all have a great stake in fairness and solemnity when our throats are being cut. I certainly didn't say that. Much of what I had feared about the attractive woman was coming out earlier and more unmistakably than I could have hoped. My job was to save his face so he could learn in his own way. As I said, he was a prudent man, sometimes brilliant; he didn't need a preacher.

Again I remembered some of the ways I had tried to persuade my first wife to stay. I do think of myself as a loyal man, although others may see it as passivity or lack of imagination. In either case, I too became a great fan of solid virtues; she was either too guilty herself or too diplomatic to remind me how I served my career far more faithfully than I had served my family. It seems even more pathetic in retrospect. Having become acquainted with myself over many years, however, I am not surprised.

It is this same getting acquainted I was hoping to foster. Of course getting acquainted with the woman, but more with himself. There are special features of getting acquainted with oneself. Perhaps the most striking is proximity: we go everywhere together, except in sleep and madness. Still we are forgetful companions, often losing sight of one another, assuming that a passing interest is really ours. We can also be deeply divided against ourselves, going about with widely separated and disowned parts. That is not so great a lack of self-possession as when we lose ourselves altogether. We can literally lose our minds the way we lose our wallets. You know you have lost it because you can't find it in the expected place; there seems nothing to take control of your thoughts or summon memories. A wallet or a mind is also known to have been lost when it appears in unexpected places. I realize I've been without my wallet all day when at night I see it on the bureau. Or the mind might speak from an unexpected place, as hallucinating voices do from the sky or your foot. Getting acquainted becomes very unsettling. But, then, getting acquainted with ourselves is always unsettling.

Going around so intimately with ourselves, we frequently quarrel, reprimand, advise. Sometimes we hear the dialogue out loud, as when people mutter to themselves or curse or goad themselves in sports. Many of the discussions, like domestic quarrels in general, are unreasonable. Now and then I play tennis next to an extremely sane and able man who gives himself amazing grief for missing shots that I, as a former tennis teacher, know he could never hit. That is, not only mad people carry on this way. Getting acquainted with ourselves therefore asks much in the way of patience and forgiveness. The musician blamed himself for failures I could not lay at his doorstep. He saw the most everyday anxieties and low spirits as signs of deficit or disease. Perhaps people talk this way only to therapists, but I hear much of the inevitable static of human life—the ups and downs of everyday life—put forward very gravely.

The proximity of our relationship with ourself is doubtless one reason for the quarrelsomeness. Oddly, another is our unfamiliarity. The sane tennis player seems unacquainted with himself. At least in this one respect he is like someone who has lost his sense of humor; rather than being amused, he is surprised. You would think that, after such long proximity, we would all be better acquainted with ourselves. Yet it is common for husband and wife to spend forty years together and not understand each other. We can be even more remote from ourselves, partly because we only watch ourselves in mirrors and may not see the mirrors of others. This is another of the great powers of psychotherapy. Two people sitting opposite each other hour after hour in a largely unchanging place stabilizes those reflections, lets them settle and be seen. May no one be critical or impatient. It is hard to see yourself. One other reason goes by unnoticed.

Both Joyce and Freud tried to make the inner voice continuous and public; this joyful and interesting task was not received joyfully. Again, getting acquainted with ourselves is unsettling. There are forbidden thoughts, but also commonplace ones. I have often remarked that when the psychotherapist opens us up, he finds what the surgeon finds, all the usual organs. The unique contour of our being only shapes a universal content. It is hard to see ourselves because the individuality we may prize is hardly there. We are all much more alike than we are different. Looking in the mirror we see everyone.

The patient carried himself around with growing fatigue and, more happily, with growing familiarity. I like my doctors to be confident; no one wants nervous surgeons. Even in the face of disaster they should be able to relieve pain. I try to be confident myself. As I said, he made it easy, what with his prudence and sensitivity. Now he revealed a reason for even greater confidence. I had begun to think the attractive woman would outlast us all. I had tried not to be impatient; he had to decide. I even devised schemes for him to win her back or discourage other suitors. Now I think he decided. He had always worked alone, avoiding close competition. The other suitors may have been the last straw. He stopped visiting her and didn't return her calls.

The familiarity I sought for him was, first, a dispossession. The attractive woman had dispossessed him. They had become acquainted; then he dispossessed himself of her. He returned home to find himself again dispossessed; he was no longer the adored musician. And his wife was more eager to get acquainted than he was.

He held himself aloof, ostensibly to further his teaching of music. In fact he did that with success, but his personal thrust seemed toward me. Hour after hour he challenged me to find him empty and purposeless, passive and drifting. I thought he was saying, "Of course I must annex and possess others—see how little there is of me." It served nothing to tell him that. What we had to do was uncover or develop what he was not experiencing. But he didn't want to get acquainted—he was tired of himself.

It was not like meeting a man with a dangerous secret, who must always change the subject when the subject is himself. There are many like that. This man talked readily about himself. The problem was in what he said. I wondered if he wanted me to contradict him, to talk about the good things. He had two depressed parents who could see no good in each other or themselves. He said everyone in the family whined. He hated whining, but that was all he felt like doing. It felt like his turn.

One of my teachers liked to say, "Many neuroses you have to bore to death." I objected to that. The vision of a life spent boring anything or anyone to death had no appeal. I should have looked more closely at my teacher. She was not bored and certainly was not boring. She was a bit of a possessor herself; she didn't "wait on" people, however much she might wait them out. In her exquisite Viennese way she reflected repetitions back, without rancor or great reassurance. She appeared faintly amused. And when she spoke you listened. The musician would have whined, but he would also have wondered.

I didn't want to shorten "his turn." I did want him to wonder, in particular, whether his having bought me—having enlisted and paid me—entitled him to quite the degree of ownership he seemed to imply. The feelings of sadness and drifting paralyzed him, he said. He'd then fall silent. I was meant to do something, by his reading of the contract. I didn't want to address that directly; it could seem an attack, a counter-whining, the old family game. Often I'd say, "Where does one find the courage?" I meant that it's hard, courage is needed, but where does it come from? The idea of courage did come from me; courage itself had to come from somewhere else. Where could that be?

Later I will speak of giving people credit, the way banks do. I did give him credit for the many abilities he had, but I wanted to shake the possession he felt of me. This is not to say he could not take me with him, wherever he went, like himself. I would be happy to become part of him. But I wasn't going to do the work myself. He reminded me of an old steamboat story. The steamboat was little, its whistle very large. When the whistle blew, the little steamboat stopped. It didn't have power enough for both. The patient was like that: when he complained, he stopped. Again, where would the new power come from?

He was waiting me out. I had to hold him until he got moving on his own because, without me, he might possess someone new who would try to do it for him. The whistle was his way of gaining possession of people; it had held his wife. It also frightened him. For one thing, it sounded so much like his parents that he thought he must be as helpless as they seemed. I wanted to transform his anxiety back into what anxiety really is, a warning signal, a mobilization of resources being readied for battle. The anxious mind scans the battlefield, seeing dangers, weighing risks, sensibly occupied with what may happen. For all the confidence great commanders show, they are very busy people. I suspect that complacency was Napoleon's downfall. The plump little emperor lost his unrivaled attention to detail. Maybe he thought he was invincible. The lesson is: keep those who are anxious about anxiety off the battlefield, perhaps away from human challenges altogether.

I wanted the patient to endure his fear, use it as a signal of danger, outface the danger, above all recognize what he could do: to be neither possessor nor possessed. Many years ago I had a brief affair with fame, but she left me for another man. He had just experienced something similar. Yet he might still succeed in possessing me or his wife. I wanted each pair to be both separate and together, an intimacy without conquest.

One of the peculiarities of marriage is how it copies the relationship we have with ourselves. There is proximity, frequent quarrelsomeness, and often striking unfamiliarity. Further, we would like to respect our spouses and ourselves, and this extends to liking and loving each other. In many cultures it is a central hope, to treat each other as we would be treated ourselves. How we treat each other in psychotherapy is as important as how we learn to see each other and ourselves. The therapist's responsibility therefore goes beyond treating the patient well; he must make it possible for the patient to treat him well too. And this also extends into marriage. My patient and his wife needed to learn to treat each other well.

There is one aspect of learning to treat each other well that we practiced together. He was very careful with me; perhaps I was always a bit of the hired gun. There was only the matter of his seeking to possess me some, and that was subtle. Its clearest indication was not jealousy or outright demands. It was more like sitting on a doorstep. I wondered if he was in part paying me back, perhaps for not being emotionally generous enough with him. The sense I had of his power did give me confidence that he could be let alone. But what I saw as an expression of confidence might be experienced as an example of neglect. So I spoke at length about how much he had accomplished, in his learning and teaching, in dealing with the woman, in his attention to his children, even to his wife. I said I thought his prospects were considerable. He had, for example, a measure of both prudence and creativity rarely found together. Whether in relation to my remarks or not, he assisted his wife in finding a much-desired job she had earlier feared to seek. I had always tried to keep his interests foremost, but now I was speaking more of his abilities. This was an acknowledgment with which he was genuinely unfamiliar. But neither my praise nor his assistance to the wife should have possession as an object; nor should any of the parties be taken advantage of. Both needed to be statements from separate and independent bodies. How did I know this was happening?

We experience acts of possession or taking advantage as being pulled out of shape—psychologically swollen with conquest or impinged upon and depleted. The experience is recorded bodily; in order to determine its occurrence, you consult your gut. "How does that make me feel?" The intimate relation of body and feeling, discreetly in sensations, more holistically in feelings themselves, means the self is significantly a bodily self, so that we experience invasions of our psychological being in its bodily vessel. Often in the past I felt pulled in his direction, by the yearning and helplessness; I felt myself becoming a prosthesis of his cunning. I had to settle down against the pull. Now it subsided; he would laugh a little feeling himself do it.

The patient was like all of us in approaching novelties of psychological life with a gesture of avoidance. He was used to possessing. It was not something he thought of doing or not doing; it simply happened. He did not "feel able" to relate separately; he lacked, it has been said, the affective competence, which meant dropping his half-spoken belief: I can't stay by myself; I must have that person. He must go right up to the novelty of separation and stay with it.

So there I was, right in front of him, seemingly ready to be had, yet just a trifle elusive. Could he get along at once with and without me? Of course the success of the exercise depended as much on my not possessing him as the other way around. I had to be willing to leave him alone, even as I sat there large as life. The exercise is a good deal more dramatic than the words suggest; a great deal is at stake. And the subtlety of the determinations! Some prefer rockclimbing or high-energy physics or going to the moon. I like this.

We wait on the world and the world, now and then, waits on us. The opportunities we have passed right by, many as silent as the night, are slowed in therapy, stretched out to an hour or a week and then visited again and again. Even so they may slip by, these chances to be different, to make a different world. I listen to the rain outside, falling on both the just and the unjust; a gray sky closes down the world, only yesterday blue and limitless. The patient was always very conscious of the weather. He read his fate in it, like a Roman general peering at the entrails of a goat. I am superstitious myself. I knock on wood. It is a way of acknowledging the randomness of the world. We were at the opposite pole now, seeking to impose a change. Could we be alone together?

I can't say I know, even now. I did come to experience being with him differently, less tugging, less a weight, but closer too. He also spoke of living easier with his wife, where she had once grated on him terribly. Perhaps he will return some day and I can sit with him again. I will not *know*, even then. The work is like family practice everywhere, new problems, new excitements. One is not cured of life.

7 ~ The Struggle for Existence

I must be both as free and as compliant as I dare. Each side serves the other. Unless I comply, I cannot be free, for revolt is at most the beginning of freedom. And unless I am free, I cannot fully comply, because what I do with others will be forced. We cannot live without people or with them, for they are always different. The supreme individuals I have known possess both the strength of a great freedom and the gentleness of unforced compliance.

You hire the doctor to paint a picture of the ideal—sought for, seldom reached—against which we sense what is wrong. The patient assumes the doctor knows what health is. Relatively complete and describable for the physical body, this ideal construction still struggles to birth for psychological being. Freedom and compliance are two of its elements.

The patient could hardly drag herself through the door. She had not risen so much as rolled out of bed into the arms of an angry, desperate husband. Internists, psychoanalysts, pharmacologists, and psychotherapists all treated her, and she was still in bed. She said her mind was a nightmare of curses, recriminations, regrets, and fruitless efforts to undo the regrets. Yet she said it all calmly, as if she were recounting a dream just passed. For all the madness of her thoughts, I never knew her to sound bizarre, incomprehensible, or out of touch. If she had a fury, it was a fury to explain.

I was lucky to be called in so late because the failure of the others suggested that I work in a different way. They had studied her brain and her unconscious, her chemicals and her complexes. There didn't seem anything left to study but her situation and herself; we needed to look closely at the world she lived in. I was also in no hurry to explain, suspecting her fury to explain was partly the attitude of her doctors carried over into the illness itself. Her husband was a lawyer. I wondered whether his mind was as busy. I wondered too if I could understand her without understanding him; each carried one of those two opportunities, compliance and freedom, so I begin with her and end with him.

In the pantheon of medicine and psychology it is a humble task, this study of situations, what was once called *psychiatrie de concierge*. French professionals used that disdainful phrase, suggestive of a task beneath science, to shame Americans doing what Americans do best, the practical and managerial. Nevertheless, Harry Stack Sullivan and the behaviorists, family therapists and marriage counselors—so many wanted to know what you would have seen if you had been there. Who was doing what to whom?

Likewise the concierge studies the guests. The concierge needs to decide who will pay and who will steal. My hotel is very small, the visits are short, and people usually come alone. But most of the guests keep returning, and I am the only concierge. I seem to attract people who are generally innocent, poor managers of difficult situations. Whether that is true or my perception, I don't know. Still it is a strong impression, suggesting that people visit me because life at home is hard.

The patient was very concerned with what the lawyer-husband thought. Further, she was often confused as to where his thoughts left off and hers began. It was as if he had taken up a position like a conscience in her mental life, a semi-independent center of opinions and recriminations with judgelike powers. Early in their relationship he had established rules to govern her behavior and a system of punishments to enforce them. He had not so much ordered as argued them into existence. The rules were complicated, like many legal rules, and there were exceptions, reparations, and processes of appeal. At first the patient had liked this system, since it settled her mental life, which, she said, had been drifting and lax. It also seemed an improvement over the rules her father and mother decreed, the ten commandments plus a set of family customs that included an almost religious belief in wheat germ and vitamins. These rules made life at once perfectly simple and utterly separate from any particular interests or observations of the patient's own.

The two plans had in common her compliance. She accepted in a good-natured spirit with a hearty willingness to make things work and enthusiasm for her husband's cleverness. She was not inclined to wonder about either her own rights or the general status of his beliefs. They seemed to her eccentric, but she carried a commonsense approach to ideas in general: there were a great many, people argued, there were no obvious solutions; one sensibly puts the whole matter to one side. It took about ten years of marriage for her own interests to surface.

These appeared autonomously, first as spasms or nervous tics, apparently from nowhere. Neurologists were consulted, medicines prescribed; they subsided. Then she became lethargic, first briefly, later for weeks on end. Into this lethargy disconnected thoughts would come, frequently of curses or thoughts of someone dying and then ideas of performing rituals and enduring punishments by way of compensation. At the time I first saw her, most of her waking life was concerned with these thoughts. It might seem remarkable that this intelligent woman did not report the correspondence between the plague of thoughts and the rules of governance her husband had imposed. Probably she had bought into, or more accurately had been sold into, those rules so completely that she had no perspective of her own. She had come to see the world as he did, legally ordered, divided into right and wrong, properly punished. Freedom was the right to do what you were supposed to do. Her own viewpoint did not so much emerge as sputter up. The slave became restive, her muscles twitched; then a mood emerged, against her general affability; finally curses, a kind of swearing under her breath. Curiously such signs of revolt had been noted in the husband's legal system, as if he had sensed, perhaps within himself, the possibility and decreed suitable retributions.

Samuel Butler once remarked that the public mind is owned just as the land is owned, so that the writer wanting to gain a piece of that mind must buy, marry, or fight. Truth will not come out on its own; the struggle for existence extends to mind and heart. The patient's mind was owned. In her case, it had been all three, bought, married, and fought for, by the husband. So what chance did I have?

Even when she had gained insight, into the similarity of her obsessing thoughts and his compelling claims, the insight would vanish, overpowered. For a moment she would feel herself lift above the competing claims and enter a world free and uncluttered. In the course of the treatment, these moments became longer and more continuous. Whole days passed in a spirit she remembered from years ago. Then the nightmare mood and ideas would return, seemingly for no reason. Even when she seemed to accept the idea of his possession of her, the specific ways he encroached would elude her. She could no more recognize his psychological power in action than a muscle understands the nervous system. She could agree with me, as she agreed with him; there was still no independent center of control.

You would not have believed this meeting her. She was a large woman with a noble head. Natural grace accompanied a regal bearing. Free of the nightmare she seemed sunny, at home, quick-witted. She certainly was a prize to capture. Those vulnerable to psychological possession signal it by a readiness to please; the first movement is to open, not to close. Doctors love these patients. They obey, they put out their arms, they pay. Inside the mind a wonderful peace reigns. Order, harmony, a belief in the essential goodness of people, the eagerness to join in and be accepted, these are the inward content of the outward sunny form.

In *Memoirs of Hadrian,* Marguerite Yourcenar imagines the mind of that great emperor as he went about laying the groundwork of public order. Hadrian's first motive was not power, vast as his power was, but freedom, and freedom needs power. He wanted his subjects to be free to comply, which precludes tyranny and slavery. The fundamental principle of his reign could be seen as respect, respect for both the play of his own impulses and the play of his subjects'. Yourcenar describes him most aptly by what he is not: "a good soldier, but not a great warrior; a lover of art, but not the artist which Nero thought himself to be at his death; capable of crime but not laden with it." There is a curious lightness to this man's imperial being. He is slow to respond when a problem has ample margins; much can be left to work itself out, if capably watched. You feel in the descriptions of Roman rule and customs that its people do not crowd one another. Edmund Burke said something similar about the best practice of the British Empire: it was rule by "salutary neglect."

There was no neglect in the husband's rule, except neglect of her soul. He seemed terrified. Every frontier was closely watched and instantly defended. It was as if his boundaries touched every physical surface of the house and belongings. A matchbox moved on his bureau was noted, straightened, and her carelessness attacked. Once a tiny door usually shut was half ajar; he saw it at once. He was like a general in a battle going badly; he sensed the slightest loss of control. If you have ever worked closely with someone who is very afraid, you know how contagious that fear becomes. Certainly she was afraid of disturbing his frontiers; she came to fear those frontiers crossing sharply behind her own. He was perceptive; she would sometimes find him half talking to himself in thoughts she was having herself. His fear of infidelity had a curious form; he seemed to fear it only when he didn't have the same thought himself. It was acceptable to admire a man he himself admired, which is the opposite of the norm. I believe he meant: only thoughts different from mine are dangerous.

He said he loved her; he could curl up beside her in a comforting way. She said it sometimes felt as if he curled up inside her, perhaps like a child waiting to be born. It was pleasant. Later this interior presence would turn malignant. She sometimes awoke, having fallen asleep beside him, wondering if the voice she had heard was a dream or the actual critical shout so often made. This is the surest sign of mental possession, the loss of a clear boundary between inside and outside. The frontier has been crossed; the enemy is within.

The mental possessor stakes out his position just as an invading army captures towns and sets itself up within them. Already existent centers of ideals and prohibitions function like physical redoubts. The patient found the husband's influence fanning out from his gradual possession of her values; he became her conscience. I believe she was so vulnerable in part because her parents' capture of the same points of influence had been another uneasy tyranny. She had accepted very few of the earlier rules, which came to seem foolish, even barbaric. Yet she had not been able to recapture the points of influence for herself. As I said, the husband's rules were at first a happy substitution. But again she ended up unable to identify whole-heartedly with what he believed. The result was a civil war in which she was the battleground.

The previous efforts at treatment failed, I believe, because the battle was not engaged. On the one hand, she could not defend herself. On the other, her therapists did not confront the husband, either in his person or in his mental repre-sentations. They did not make themselves felt against her invaders. There was a still deeper problem. At least one of the therapists was unwilling to put himself forward as a new repre-sentation of values to be made her own. He told me explicitly that this is not the doctor's job. Yet I don't see how the therapeutic job can be done without doing just that. How could she be freed unless the points of influence were first captured by another force, a force willing to abandon them when the search for her own values began? I have never known an instance in which someone could generate alone the force necessary to recapture self-possession.

I didn't want to impose myself on her. I believed her symptoms sprang in part from the husband's imposing himself on her. Noting that did not free her, although it helped. Nor could she leave him. Such a solution would not be useful until she had a mind of her own. She came to hear me as she heard her parents and husband. I suppose I might have used that power to effect a divorce. But would that be what she wanted? Wouldn't she fall under another influence if she escaped his and mine? It might be that her marriage was the ideal place in which to begin the exercise of her own powers. Perhaps she could use my power to offset the husband's and find her own way between.

It began to happen. She sometimes told the husband what I said. The husband deplored this as he listened. I became a voice in her home. A space was opening among the powers. Now and then she called on God, supplication. It was not a turn to me or the husband, perhaps more to the parents who took their rules from God. I welcomed this the way one welcomes division among one's enemies: a chance appears for new alliances. Her opportunity was different. It has been suggested that personal consciousness arises with the death of gods; personal agency waits upon the waning of supreme authorities. Her calling on God was an admission. She told me she had always believed he was with her, that she had done what he asked and would therefore support her. The new insight into her revolt carried with it despair, but it was not only despair of escaping the husband; she also felt deserted by God. So the yearning for God was a sign of his distance. In earlier god-saturated times, deities were all around; there were no personal arguments. Her yearning for God suggested the emergence of a personal consciousness. She was deserted, under siege; she called out; the voices that called back seemed less and less godlike, mine, the husband's, perhaps also the sound of silence she said she heard after prayer.

First she filled the empty space with belief in me; I was to be her new god. For a while she felt cheerful and clear. She cut down the visits, then said goodbye. A few months passed, and the twitching or the cursing or the lethargy returned. She could not live with me; she could not live with the husband. Where was she to go?

Over and over we come to the same point, like runners gasping to exceed their times. "Times" is the word because it is the same time after time, until our time runs out. Time sets the pace and the limit. What breaks the mark? First there is a sensing of where we want to get. Then it is a matter of heart, of affective strength, competence to carry oneself above and beyond. You would not have thought she could walk there, much less run. That was the challenge. She did not fling it down, this uncertain woman. I flung it down for her. We must make her world. We must guard her frontiers, shape her own space. There was still time.

I couldn't tell if she heard me. I have learned not to ask for that. One goes forward unaccompanied for a while, hoping the path is right and someone will follow. Here is both the glory and the horror of all conceptions. I knew what I was trying to do: set her up in her own place. But did she want it, could she do it? Was this the problem at all? Waking at four in the morning with such responsibilities, I don't sleep well. I know what I tell myself. Go forward a little, see if she follows; wait and see if she leads. Have I set something in motion of her own?

Her own, what she owns. It is on such a recognition that our work turns. How do we know what the other wants? The uncertain woman presented the problem in her own way. She often spoke as if she were watching a movie. The lights would go on, reality would reappear, the horror show was over. The differences she felt were crisp and decisive. She was like a visual artist whose perceptual genius lies wholly apart from the individual's thinking or life. I long suspected she was drawing this dramatic contrast for my benefit, to show the extent and power of her obedience. Mental life, in my experience, only exhibits such sharp contrasts when subject to art and presentation; it is otherwise closer to the wandering vagueness she generally lived in. She was an artist of her illness, and this long and torturous production was, in fact, her own. I played a part, her parents and husband still larger parts. True, she was not the sole director or the author, and her plight was real. But many have lived the same fate without drama or protest or a moment of medical attention. In her case it was building a ghastly story out of what was in fact a ghastly life.

And she set fine traps for doctors. The apparatus of diagnoses and complexes has no place for the brilliant rendering she put forth. It reminded me of the much-neglected correction some tried to give Freud's theory of the dream, to his insistence on the dreamwork's censorship or disguise of wishes. Instead, dreams were taken to render, often shatteringly, the actual situations of people's lives. An isolated, friendless woman dreamed of being in a refrigerator inside a boxcar deep under the Arctic ice. My patient's mood and symptoms could also be understood as renderings of her meager and embattled existence. Reference to diseases or to a disguised unconscious led attention away from that existence. In fact her husband had summoned the chemists and analysts. Was he protecting himself?

If the dramatic suffering of the illness was her own, indeed her own creation and feelings, I was in fresh danger. Stating that the illness was hers carried a freight of blame: once again something principally hers was bad; her existence was no more than a sickness. Instead I had to render the "sickness" as the expression of her health, celebrate the exactness and power with which she had depicted her existence. I found this very hard. At first she thought I was caricaturing her, making fun of illness, or patronizing her, in the manner of someone who admires a smile on a slave. I wasn't successful until I had myself found a way to render her plight, so that she could see and hear what I had seen and heard. She had been inside her own production and could not experience it from outside. She needed to join the audience of her own life.

Then she might begin to sense the strength in her weakness. I would be her interpreter, translating sickness into health, showing that apparent weakness, what seemed a profound malaise, was a vivid statement of imprisonment. I would already have taken what felt to her an unbelievable step: that she should have something to celebrate, particularly something of her own. This struck in the face of a lifelong servility. Granted it was a servility disguised by her regal appearance, by her enthusiastic endorsements, in fact by everything except the illness itself. But the illness was a disguise; at least it had fooled her keepers. I didn't know, though, to what extent the keepers were themselves in thrall to her servility; certainly the husband was.

Perhaps the stake so many had in power and obedience forbade their reading a convincing statement for what it was. This was a chilling thought, with its forecast of the reception such a document as mine would get.

Even the most complacent, even those most secure in the exercise of their power, must feel a distant tremor as the movement for respect and independence mounts. They will not believe, as the husband for a long period did not, that their freedom too is being prepared. It was one of the great joys of this treatment to see him change as much as she did. Almost to the end he fought her. But the effort became sporadic; by the end he simply sputtered, as her first symptoms of independence had sputtered. The joy was in the freedom secured. He gave up guarding his frontiers and skirmishing behind hers. Whole days would pass without an attack or reprimand. And it was not because he was frightened or defeated. He was too busy to notice. Others finding him more human also filled his time. Her memories were too bitter and wretched for her to love him wholeheartedly, but she could love him some, as she had once.

I have known that man in many forms, some my own. A patient I saw almost twenty years ago resembled him. This man, a doctor, came to see me because he wanted to write. He said he liked the way I wrote and thought I could help him. So we began with an impersonal task, as is often the case, only entering the work deeply when his wife walked out. This surprised him. She had not complained, and now there was no persuading her to return. God knows he tried everything, including an attempt to like hockey, which she adored. He was a loyal soul and adaptable, in awkward, halting ways. I came to believe he had never felt a close part of the world around him. He described himself as a bookish man, doing his best to compensate for his own uncomfortable aloofness by gathering power, money, the loyalty of his colleagues. Later in our work he told me he would have traded it all for a more casual way in the world. He loved to watch young people walking together down the street; it was the image that most excited him. The unselfconsciousness, the easy banter, the open, trusting way they looked at each other seemed remote from everything he did. He couldn't recall anyone looking at him that way.

He too was on guard. His was a reflective consciousness; it took in at once both himself and the other. What he envied the young people was their seemingly undivided attentiveness, their giving themselves so freely away. How safe they must feel. And their directness appeared to carry no aggressiveness or hostility. It seemed that everyone he looked at aroused his fear and often repugnance. He would love to look into the young people's eyes without fear, openly, but he had come to expect from strangers either surprise or disdain.

Once he heard himself described as a "nerdy, temperamental man." Watching a film made at a party, he squirmed to see his awkwardness and the waves of obsequiousness or anger that swept across his face. He asked me if I could make him an easier person, more lovable and steady, less frightened and demanding. I thought to myself: he is shy, but there's no shy acceptance; he can't accept this singular existence. He often awoke in the morning wanting to die. I didn't blame him. He was so fearful of life, above all of people, that the only alternatives seemed conquest or death. And he had come by his fear honestly; on two occasions his young existence had been unpredictably destroyed; he would have been a fool not to be afraid. Yet surely, I thought, he can reach closer to an acceptance, the shy part he had already.

The complacent lawyer I described earlier owned his exist-ence; this man barely tolerated his, though at moments of conquest he could seem very proud indeed. I would not persuade him of the bountifulness of life; he knew too much for that. I could give him an experience or, more exactly, a relationship in which acceptance of life's vagaries was the theme. He might then carry that with him forever; I might become the representative of life as it is tolerable. I am enough like the fearful man to make that an adventure for both of us. Perhaps we could persuade each other.

Honestly undertaken, the work of making lives together is always an adventure. Entering a relationship is like entering a forest. However companionable we feel, however stirred by a common purpose, the mystery of our two beings and the further mystery of their intermingling close around us like the trees. Challenges of an unfamiliar noise or a branching path immediately summon particular fears, our resentment of fears, our demands for support. The deeper we go, the longer the history of challenge and response is laid down, the more we are tempted to conclude about each other and undertake measures of repair and reprisal. We cannot help being driven apart at the very moment we are drawn together, so unpredictable are the reflections thrown off from one to the other. It is partly that we may not like what we think we see; more important, we may lose the capacity to feel that what we see has different meanings, different possibilities of being. What once prompted our crea-tivity, as we set out, now prompts our concluding.

The forest guide we thought we needed is soon partly lost too, in a relationship that must be to some extent unique. Then we assess the guide's helpfulness not by the measure of his knowing the paths or the destination but by a measure of inventiveness, the capacity to keep a level and lively head when our own is addled and depressed. It is therefore good that we do not see each other all the time. The guide needs to disappear and return refreshed, maybe with a new perspective.

Before he saw me, the fearful man received a long course of therapy directed at his origins. He learned much of where he came from and what had happened. He said he did not change; in fact he often felt depressed, because the guide kept referring failings to him and looking back at the long muddled path behind. He told me he wanted to go forward and be different. I was thankful for what had been uncovered, but agreed.

He did something that the stately woman's husband did too. When his wife was cheerful or merely agreeable, her value sank; his longing went elsewhere. When she seemed distant or cold, he feared losing her. The contrast was very sharp, between wanting her to leave and hating her to go. He was like a furnace with a thermostat: when the room got cold, he got warm, and the reverse. I believe his purpose was also like the thermostat's to maintain an even temperature. He was afraid of both passion and desertion. Perhaps the temperature was set too low for the wife's comfort, so she left. I wanted to reset his thermostat or throw it out altogether. And he did to me what he did to his wife. When I praised him, he turned aside. If he thought I was preoccupied, he became solicitous. I was held, but at arm's length: a cool, stiff control, again the shyness but not the acceptance. He wanted to control what one can control only by reducing psychological life to the straightest, narrowest channels. His was the image of a mechanical man, ordering a life he had come to fear and often abhor.

On the whole I think the wife did better with her husband than I did with my patient, but we worked in comparable ways.

Each of us had a power the other lacked. The once-servile wife could terrify the husband, now afraid of losing her. Once she left to spend a night with a girlfriend; he was good as gold for a week. I had the less dramatic advantage of being entrusted with a small but perhaps acceptable slice of my patient's existence. We could experiment with various degrees of closeness, warmth, and forthright hostility to increase his emotional range. Both the wife and I were exercising our respective charges, in the same way that joint doctors increase the range of motion in a limb. She could take him through a new set of paces at home; my paddock was smaller but more comfortable. She had the advantage of power but also its attendant danger of enforced obedience. I was less powerful; yet what I found might be his own.

Both men felt terribly exposed to their singular existences. The extensive success each achieved did not reduce that exposure; in fact there was more to fear, in the same way rich people have larger and larger investments to protect. Paradoxically, it was their marital defeats that saved them. It is a hard lesson. I have seldom found that success improves anyone, and many good people have been ruined by it. We can imagine a developmental psychology of defeat: the capacity to survive frees psychological life from its otherwise abject dependence on results and applause; it breaks the thermostat by which we respond to the world's shifting weather. Success has the opposite effect, of increasing our excited dependence, so that we are drawn further and further outside ourselves.

But there is no wishing for defeat. This is because defeat may obliterate people whose only hold on life comes through success. The doctors of souls gain their central importance here.

The broken psychological life must be held, time found to reconnect the scattered pieces, a new existence made.

The struggle for psychological existence is as ferocious and unrelenting as the struggle for food and space and the propagation of the species. It is marked by a curious invisibility as long as physical measures preoccupy us or the predators have their way. Freedom and compliance secure their importance as yardsticks of health whenever human existence is misshapen by either power or resignation. Then we see freedom turned into power and compliance into resignation. Depression, noted today almost everywhere, bespeaks that resignation. As the servile woman overcame both her oppression and her depression, she entered on a freedom that allowed her to comply on her own with a husband also lighter and freer of a burden of power carried in fear.

The Real

8 ~ The Naked

In the older state mental hospitals, one meets people who seem psychologically naked, who wear their hearts on their sleeves. The hospitals function as a kind of armor—crude, often uncomfortable, hopelessly restricting—which protects them from the world they entered and left unequipped. Coming into life requires dressing against climates bitterly cold or burningly close.

You see them walking the spacious hospital grounds alone, many whispering to themselves or talking out loud, casting frightened or angry glances, at once pathetic and proud. No outcasts of far eastern isles ever seemed so distant from our images of community. Only in the great cities do we meet the same isolation, anger, and fear, as if the extremes of failure and success had joined hands. Indeed, the hospital failures—of the two extremes—walk the more salubrious space on the broad, quiet lawns, under great trees. Someone told me once that even the pigeons are quieter there. If only the inner voices would stop.

When the interns and residents enter those hospital grounds, track down the scattered patients, coax them to sit and talk, the newcomers are at first appalled. Snarling, terrified, wrapped in stories of assault and madness, talking ragtime if they talk at all, the patients seem inhuman. It is an extraordinary fact that three or four months later, many of these odd couples, doctors and patients, are the best of friends.

What happens is this: when the doctors are willing to listen, tolerate insult and rejection, when, above all, the new doctors can be with others and leave them alone, the crude dress of hostility and bizarreness falls away and a naked soul speaks. Not smooth, suave speech, not my proud lawyer's sequential and appropriate speech, but the sounds we humans make when the place seems safe and the ear friendly and attentive. It is wonderful, this contrast between first appearances and the warmth of friendship, between horror and acceptance. And it is most wonderful for emerging where you might least expect it.

The two people make each other feel good. The young therapists almost stumble on the person in the patient, and the patients are no less delighted to find a person in their educated and ambitious helpers. Here the substitution of real persons suppressed for images goes forward with a rapidity I have seen outstripped in only one circumstance. It was an embarrassment when I met it first. I was then the ambitious young doctor, presenting to my colleagues my patients' bizarre nakedness with all the ruthless, descriptive rigor I had learned in medical school. The important thing was not to overlook any single bit of pathology. When the most thorough of us finished, even mildly psychotic persons came out as monsters; images of disease clung around them. The most lurid novelist never suppressed the whole person more completely. My embarrassment appeared after one of these presentations. The patient was ushered in, sat down next to my chief, and the two talked. Many times their heads came together, and you might have thought two old friends were recalling old times. Where was my monster now? It was not because the two were discussing neutral topics or incidental matters; it was love, loss, despair suffered together. My patient had been replaced. Years ago a Harvard graduate student spent a year on a Yale psychiatric ward, pretending to be a patient, so that he could write a book. I thought maybe Yale was paying us back.

But it happened too many times for that to be true. Moreover, it was not supposed to happen at all. If psychoses were brain diseases or the product of unconscious forces and primitive defenses, what was happening here? Part of the psychoses had disappeared. Nothing in the prevailing theories then and little in the theories now explained those interviews. People laughed when Sullivan said, "No one is psychotic when they talk to me." It was a commonplace to claim that was because Sullivan was more psychotic than the patients. But no one ever called my old chief psychotic. Besides, some of us figured out what he did and passed it on. That may have been one reason why those young therapists and their patients could become friends.

They made each other feel good. How did that happen? It is a question you would expect any doctor to answer, even without medicines to ease the particular pain. But the naked souls flitting under the great trees would not expect it. They had given up whatever hopes they had years before. Other doctors often made them feel bad, sicker, more different, like the monster I created. So what did my old chief do, or those new doctors with their new friends?

For one thing they were all very conscious of how others "make them feel." All three of these words are right. There is force in the feeling-relation; we can't easily step aside or correct it. The beautiful image of my patient with the chestnut hair made me feel good; part of me did not want to see it fade. No doubt my eager pursuit of every ounce of sickness in that poor soul years ago made her feel bad; I helped to create what I described. This has been said many times: there are no patients, only patients and observers; there are no babies, only babies and mothers. We also know we can make ourselves feel good. The ever-renewed literature of self-help depends on that, just as the need for it arises when others, or ourselves, have made us feel bad. The sad soul hears itself cry out to itself, "Oh peace, give me peace." Many of the naked souls in the great hospitals dare not say even that; they hear only vicious voices calling them mad or shouting, "Kill, kill, kill!"

The two persons had stumbled on one another. Each person being with the other made the other feel good—not by a beautiful image, not even by admiration of the beautiful image, not even by acceptance of an ugly image. My earlier language was pretentious, almost ceremonial: the whole person suppressed. Is there a whole person, is it ever entirely found? How can it be suppressed? Language carries with it the baggage of many theories, much disputed. What is it harder to dispute? The two made each other feel good.

The old priest in a Camus novel, asked what he had learned in decades of hearing confession, replied, "We are all children and we are all afraid." So much for images of maturity. Person after person in long marriages speaks of this same finding of a simple other, naked souls after long trials of much else. But what do they find and what is so consoling? What does it mean to say that we find each other?

The sad souls under the great trees, so far removed from everything we seem to seek, tell at least part of the story. What each found in the other was curiously alike: fellow feelings. It is the idea that nothing is alien, an opening out into an unaccustomed safety and receptiveness. On the one hand, the patients had little to lose, we might say. On the other, what the doctors lost, in terms of their authority and prestige, suddenly seemed not worth having. The initial wariness, once the largest fear, fell away with the authority and prestige. The patients, for their part, lost some of their psychotic phenomena, so that the two sets of emblems or images, respectively of success and failure, came to seem disguises for basic simplicity and commonalty.

I was less surprised by this after I came to know socially a man who was light years away from those naked souls and their young companions. He had built a great corporation and commanded admiration and obedience from a broad community. For a while he made me feel anxious and inadequate, as if there were a question he had asked I ought to answer. He was also a very busy man, not only in his vast enterprises but in the smallest of them, such as making lunch. For all his power and authority, however, he was a servant, intent on the most extraordinary completeness of service. Someone described playing golf with him, being shepherded in every move by vigilant suggestions, often orders. The fact was that he couldn't let people alone; others came to watch him with comparable vigilance, if only to forestall. I saw him once, sitting bolt upright in the midst of his large family, watching everything, ready to move. The children probably grew up almost feeling they could hear the voice of God in their heads.

He was a great builder, of companies, families, organizations of many kinds, several homes. People who liked direction and success flocked to him. Such are the most obvious reasons he seemed so far away from the naked souls. Many of these owned nothing, not the clothes on their backs; what they built existed mainly in their heads. Busy you would never have called them, unless you know how busy humans can be controlling their thoughts or responding to internal critics. The lordly businessman was successful, by the measure of fame, money, or the number of times his name appeared in the *New York Times*. He himself would have said, quite correctly, that he tried to be helpful.

Yet, like all humans, the hospital patients and the successful man had much in common. Perhaps most startling were their attitudes toward themselves and their attitudes toward the world. They looked inward and outward through similar eyes. Both could shift abruptly between grandiose and humiliated images of themselves. It is true that the great man wore his grandiosity with a more self-conscious air than the patients sometimes wore theirs; only the latter could call themselves saviors, however much the successful man inwardly felt that way. And both were never complacent about the seemingly different worlds they lived in. For all his great courage, the successful man seemed the more afraid, afraid of what others would think of him, afraid because he had so much to lose. Once he told me that he had been braver when he was younger; now he sometimes felt afraid of everything. Yet he didn't seem to know how afraid others were, how much good relationships depend on accepting the fearfulness of others, which made him tactless and blundering.

I sit here, watching the spring winds blow the tree seeds around, down to the bricks and the asphalt. Perhaps the trees hope to sow their kingdoms everywhere. I am no different. I throw these words onto the page, hoping they will germinate in the hearts and memories of the future. Are my hopes more or less pathetic than the tree's? We are both profligate; we both mostly waste. In this respect the tree and I are different from both the naked patients and the successful man. The naked seemed to have abandoned hope of germinating anything. They were like the seeds themselves, fallen on barren places. The successful man was different in that everything he touched seemed to grow, sometimes almost monstrously, as if he commanded some extraordinary enzyme that changed the rhythms of the world.

He was not so good at building psychologically or building relationships, unless the relationships were ones of domination and submission. Rarely could he accept uncompetitive relationships. In this he was less fortunate than many of the naked souls I have known, who come more easily to less predatory ways. Much as he was a servant, the successful man used his service to dominate. By way of contrast, I will describe a man whose every gesture seemed to insist, "Hit me, dominate me."

He entered my office sideways, as if he felt unentitled to walk straight in. He made gestures of submission, as women often do. With them came an unusual sweetness, what felt like a generosity of spirit, which was repeated in the joy he described helping handicapped people. Yet he seemed in no way cloying or simpering. I felt a powerful genuineness or simplicity of character, "soul," something imageless and purely felt. This man, I thought, could never lie or get drunk or otherwise hide himself.

The clearest emanation of soul is in feeling. For this reason hysteria secures its great importance in psychological work, because hysteria reveals that feelings can be distorted and simulated. Still it is feelings that announce psychological life. As with my patient, soulful often means suffering. The soul opens itself so that we can know its suffering. It is this openness that unites the naked and the soulful. Curiously, however centered and centering the experience of soul is, it is not self-centered. Here my patient offered a telling example.

He was a tortured man. He didn't experience voices calling him names, but something close to that—a sense of wrongness, stupidity, even loathsomeness—attached to almost every move he made. There are those to whom nothing bad sticks; he was the opposite. Happiest alone, he daydreamed of worlds different from the one he lived in. So he called himself self-centered.

That was a clue. As a rule, the truly self-centered don't call themselves self-centered; they see themselves directed outward, perhaps because whatever directs them to others is notable and attracts self-congratulatory attention. The successful business-man actively served others, but it was for their good as he conceived it; he left little room for independent ideas. Others were part of his busy world; he had simply extended his own self.

In different words, what is opened is in common. The experience of soul speaks for anyone as much as for itself. It is what human beings share, like breath and blood. This awareness of a common human fund prompts all those transcendental and metaphysical statements, for instance Emerson's Oversoul from which all souls draw. That seems to me as unnecessary as claims for Overbreath or Overblood. Soul is simply what we can share.

The patient was tortured by thoughts he had about me. Unexpectedly he said he found himself thinking of touching and holding me; it was unexpected because I was only begin-ning to see how undisguised he was. He said he felt acutely disgusted with himself. I knew he felt alone and weak. How should I respond? The language of the body is perhaps the most familiar language spoken by feelings. Was I to worry about being seduced or assaulted? Worst of all, was I to increase his self-disgust at the very moment he was speaking of the need, healthy needs, to derive the strength and life he lacked in himself? But he was appalled at his painful weakness and the remedies that his mind sought.

Let the clinician worry that he or she has the strength to provide or the understanding to receive what the other trembles to ask for or mention. This could be a moment for the clinician to tremble as well, if he confuses body and soul. The patient said he thought of touching my body. I thought he wanted the vitality, the sexual excitement and power, that touching meant for him. As far as he could remember, he had never been physically intimate with another person. He even hesitated to touch his own body. How, I wondered, could such universal wishes be totally contained? How could he not want to partake of the human body, his very casing, the transmitter of experience to the mind? I believe, too, that his body wanted mine to respond physically to his desire, because desire is the great aphrodisiac, not so much our own desire as desire in the other. If I responded that way to his body's images, I could inflame his desire, perhaps even overrun his conscience. But this would also leave him crushed and distraught. What I had to do was go on speaking to his mind so terribly divided into wishes and horror at wishes.

So I said it was only natural to seek closeness with someone he hoped was stronger than he was. I wanted to celebrate his yearning, to naturalize it, while helping him find a place that the rest of him could accept. I was well placed myself to do that because I represented authority, even some measure of respectability, so that when I spoke for his yearning, not fazed by his timid seduction, he could think a little better of himself. Yet this could only be true if he thought I was speaking for him, for all his needs. If he believed the satisfaction I sought was my own, then my authority was immediately gone. If I were to say, "It's all right to enjoy sex, even for us to enjoy sex together," there would be no way for him to disclaim, or his conscience to forgive, that I might be speaking for my satisfaction alone. I would abrogate at once a confident sharing of his divided soul.

The soul emerges in conflict. Listen to any soulful song and feel the warring elements; I think of the irony and tragedy entwined in a Billie Holiday blues. Slowly we develop from such conflicts. What soul means is what we can put together, how we keep expanding from our experience, yearnings, standards, the very feeling of conflict itself. This is also why soul is so intimately sharable—these elements are part of everyone's experience. The images that struck my patient's mind as so deplorable, that split him in two as he experienced them, these alien images had to be tolerated, still better celebrated, if he was to live with himself. A whole person had been partly suppressed; he was not able to acknowledge what he needed, although he needed only what everyone needs, because he had grown alienated from himself. The very way in which the images appeared, either creeping into his mind or appearing suddenly, expressed the alienation.

My job was the usual one, to find my way past the images to the person concealed. I think of it as a slow-motion, open-field run, ducking past one threatening or enticing diversion after another. It was much the same with the successful businessman. Talking with him you felt, perhaps even more, the threats and enticements. He was handsome; one could think that was the person. He mentioned important connections;

perhaps that was the man. And the uneasy feeling he set in motion, that I was wrong or stupid, this was the greatest diversion of all—so that meeting him, simply being with him, seemed as remote as going to the Arctic.

The tortured man's diversions, on the other hand, were the opposite of respectable and appealing; they were a source of terrible shame. He greeted my translations of his images with fear and disbelief. I said of course he wanted to hold my body; it was natural and sensible, for he needed the strength and vitality he thought I had; of course he wanted to lose his isolation and weakness and be close to someone he hoped could help him. But he also felt unworthy of such help, and the problem remained: the images that entered his mind were alien to everything he took pride in, and the job of translation was as great a challenge to him as the Rosetta Stone would have been. How could these alien thoughts become part of him?

So it often is. Once another patient related an instance from ordinary life, not from the extremes of success and failure recounted here. He and his wife had a furious quarrel. Each threatened the other with lawyers. In the quiet after the storm, the wife asked, with great difficulty, "Have you ever had an affair?" He was furious again: "What difference does that make now?" She persisted. He said no, which he told me was true. She mentioned two incidents that had fueled her suspicions. It dawned on the husband that her bitterness, which so angered him, sprang from her belief that he cheated. Then he recalled that he was sometimes angry he had *not* cheated, feeling trapped by this often bitter woman. There they were, each with their secret fantasies, each angry about the same image of the husband, but she angry because she thought him unfaithful and he angry partly because he was not.

The tortured man believed I must be angry with him, as he was with himself, for the thoughts he had. If I couldn't find my way past them to the person behind, I might only confirm his theory. The husband was angry with his wife's image of him and might have escalated their quarrel further, if the irony of his position had not struck him. But how could he be truthful with her, share his fantasy, when it might rekindle her conviction? Similarly, if I told my unhappy patient I didn't want him to seduce me, his tortured sense of himself would be confirmed. How could the husband and wife share what they both already shared and what most everyone shares? Both the tortured man and the angry woman needed to make peace with their thoughts—not eliminate them (because each idea might be right) but naturalize them. For a while the husband's denial did eliminate the wife's idea, but it returned: it had not become part of their openness with each other, their soulfulness, what they carried conflictually back and forth. Things might have been easier if the husband had said, "I thought the same about you." But he had not, so she was left as the only jealous one. It might have been easier too if I could have said, "I had the same thought about you," to the tortured man. But I had not, so he was left as the only perverse one, something just as unlikely as the wife's being the only jealous one. Yet that is where we left each other.

A genuine reciprocity of feeling is soul-building because something is at once given and received; the individuals grow richer in the way banks grow richer, both giving and receiving more. Sometimes such a reciprocity arises spontaneously and is hardly noticed. Once two colleagues and I were discussing how to say goodbye to patients we liked: was it respectable to say "I love you"? (There is that "respectability" again.) We voiced many reservations. Talk moved to a wonderfully successful case of the youngest of us. This therapist had blurted out to her patient, "What you have done fills me with astonishment." The therapist, in turn, filled us with astonishment by the feeling directness and truthfulness of what she had said. There were no reservations. In their next and final meeting, the patient said to his therapist, "You fill me with astonishment." We believed that too, because the young therapist seemed to embody much of what the patient had always wanted and could not develop on his own. I thought they had filled each other, each with what the other needed, ideals the patient could begin to reach and an ideal the therapist had dreamed of, to be someone who could make a difference. They were both richer, at once giving and receiving. This is what endures.

But how was I to do that with my sad patient, the two of us staring half-embarrassed at the naked thoughts? This unhappy man was impoverished in all measures of self-worth; his bank was full of bad debts, junk bonds, relationships he felt he could not redeem, promises unsecured. He was bankrupt. He had put himself into a kind of receivership, where I was to take the tattered remains of his life and do with them what was right. He had no great hopes. If I had told him there was nothing to do, nothing worth saving, no doubt he would have thought it a just opinion and gone off to whatever fate awaited him.

Happily the psyche can be a more successful bank. We "take interest," the expression goes, when the flow of giving and receiving starts. Further, as I extended credit to the naked man, gave him credit, for example, for wanting strength and closeness, his value to himself would increase. Out of the bank of my self-regard, really a kind of vanity extended to him, would come a credit to relieve the bankruptcy. I could lend him something to repair his fortunes. In this the thought of holding my body was of particular importance: it seemed to him the clearest evidence of his bankruptcy. Surely he was not worth lending anything to. But I found in it a value he had not only overlooked but could not believe. So my lending him credit was not simply like writing a check. He had to be able to accept the credit and do something with it. At first he almost literally handed it back: "You shouldn't waste your time with the likes of me." Here the nakedness helped. I might have thought he was playing games with me, being modest, to increase his credit. But by nakedness we mean the absence of such wiles. I could easily be wrong and accumulate some bad debts, but I believed he really did think himself bankrupt. An unambivalent view toward this was important because I wanted to be able to keep extending credit with a whole heart. I saw my loan as secured by his honesty.

The naked man had lost his vanity. It was replaced by humility and those relatives of humility, shame, meekness, self-abasement, the downcast eye. Vanity always gets much the worse press of the two, with its relatives of conceit, emptiness, and pretension. Yet it is vanity that gets the world's work done. If we mean by vanity the hope of being admired, then it is vanity that sets us to all those tasks by which we dream of being remembered. In everyone claiming to do a thing for its own sake, we see the clearest vanity of all, self-regard: "This is the kind of person I want to be" or "This I can admire in myself." And, as a rule, behind that vanity is the desire to be admired by those we have most admired, the vanity of vanities.

My sad patient had few such hopes. More than happier people I know, he did do a thing for its own sake or, more accurately, because it was not like the awful things that had been done to him. He could not live with himself otherwise, and it was one reason for not giving himself credit: he was only being gentle and kind to avoid being the cruel and perverse person he thought he was. He escaped living out that identity only by the most strenuous efforts. To take pride in his accomplishments required a reconciliation with himself, specifically with those strenuous efforts and with the natural sweetness that felt to him like weakness.

The naked do not avoid their "weakness," as so many of us do. Sitting with him I often thought that nakedness is simply the absence of the capacity for self-deception. Self-deception allows happier people to be unaware of their passions. The psychotic person speaks to himself directly in the form of passionate voices, so that he is not only naked to others but to himself as well. Proust said that we can be familiar only with the passions of others. Upon ourselves our own passions react indirectly, through the imagination, which substitutes less troublesome auxiliary motives for primary ones. It is for this reason that many young doctors and patients are able to become such good friends: there is very little ordinary self-deception to get through.

Yet it is rare to find a thoroughgoing reconciliation. Perhaps it would happen more often if the requirements of training did not turn doctors to other trainings and friendships. I have seen remarkable results coming from more complete assimilations. This is what I attempted with my genuinely simple patient. The letter of credit I extended to him was admiration. Once he accepted it, the reconciliation began. Of course at first he thought I was pretending—using technical, hence insincere, means to change his mind. No, I said, I meant it; there was no place for insincerity. Naturally I could be wrong, and he was right to suspect himself, not to go about doing evil like the predators and hypocrites. Many of the naked go through life with the single object of doing no harm, like the ancient physicians. In this they may succeed, so that their lives are relatively free of the results of self-deception, intrusion and predation. Because they have not quite lost touch with the human capacity for hate and destruction, they are unhappy; but it can also make them watchful. Reconciliation does not mean the disappearance of some human trait; instead each part gets accepted as part of our selves, not always to be admired and always to be watched.

I knew he would never be vain. The self-critical voice and his own clarity were too strong for that. Nor would he be proud. But he could respect himself, although not so much as I did, for I saw him against a larger sample of human nature. One day he told me he had done something right; maybe he wasn't so stupid and useless after all. And people at work were beginning to praise him as he put himself forward with a less demeaning air. The world, I thought, is beginning to do my work for me. That is stronger and cheaper, and what I had hoped.

9 ～ Self-Deception

Feelings felt: real feelings, affectations, feelings from high drama. How are we to tell them apart? Cézanne wrote to his son, "The same subject seen from a different angle gives a subject for study of the highest interest and so varied that I think I could be occupied for months without changing my place, simply bending more to the right or left." The land-scape's consciousness reflects upon itself from differing perspectives. What if the consciousness is split into separate parts? Which is the real one?

Here I do not speak of an opening out into the unbearable and unknown but something both known and unknown to a curious state of consciousness. The self seems able to deceive itself. The real person is not so much suppressed as preoccupied, preoccupied with its images, we might expect, but also with itself. Who am I?

Therapists often ask their patients to speak of themselves. Proust, on the other hand, warns us never to speak of ourselves because that is a subject on which others' views are seldom in accord with our own and we may be adversely affected. If we possess enough effective self-esteem, our happiness is secured by looking well on what we have and askance on what others have. Proust calls this the "optics of our social perspective." As a result therapists can protect their patients' self-esteem, as well as the therapists' value in the patients' eyes, only if therapists arrange to be seen in the same way that patients see themselves. This is the operational definition of empathy: I see the world and you as if looking through your eyes.

There is considerable fascination in applying this formula to those people whose consciousness is split. How are we to know which consciousness is uppermost? Part of the appeal of hysteria for all of its observers, from the earliest times to the present, has been to follow the chase from one consciousness to the next, from one part of the body to another, from one labile affect to another, even into those depths of speaking we call the unconscious. I had such a chase with a middle-aged woman whose genuineness of expression I believed in from the start. But she spoke with at least two voices, one clipped, orderly, endlessly tactful and adaptive, the other strident and irreverent. Coming to life seemed to mean the gathering in of this second voice.

How do we deceive ourselves? How can the right hand keep its separate purposes from the left? The clever woman of different minds could have "re-minded" me how I dealt with her: I gave her what I thought was a safe place in which to question and test the conventions by which she had ordered her life. The result was a great upheaval, a change of occupation, a long period of alienation from her family, above all an abiding element of uncertainty and disorder. Was I concealing from myself the risks we ran, the price she had to pay, not only in time and money but in the whole journey across unknown ground to whatever end? True, I had been trained, done this task before, worked inside a tradition. Yet this may be the largest self-deception of all: that practice and tradition represent something reliable or replicable.

Deceiving ourselves is no more difficult than deceiving others. In fact it may be easier if we control both sides of the transaction, as when I decide not to think about painful matters. Here the woman of divided mind was not so conveniently placed. For a long time her separate minds worked independently and were mutually disdainful, one interrupting and grabbing attention from the other. Before treatment her conventional side ruled; afterward it was subordinate. For much of the period in between, there was a cacophony of voices; sometimes she thought she was going mad. Sensibly she blamed me for this state of mind. There was none of the gratitude that redeems even largely unsuccessful treatments for the self-esteem of therapists. Her conventional mind kept a decorous, cool attitude toward the proceedings. Her liberated mind, heavily criticized from the conventional side, abjured authority, rejoiced in disobedience and the freedom to hate. I had to steer the boat through wild seas: shrill abuse, threats of suicide, fresh symptoms. I can't remember a single clear sentence from her in defense of what we were doing.

How could I persist? I suppose what chiefly held the rudder was the sheer momentum of the chase, the week-to-week meetings, her willingness to talk and mine to listen. We both assumed I knew what I was doing, next to the quiet walls, the comfortable furniture, all so much more settled than any of my actual ideas or even experiences. Sometimes I felt like a small-time Columbus driven by winds that sprang up from nowhere, berthed with a mutinous crew, and emboldened by the simple fact that at least the boat had not sunk.

Landfall was to be independence. That day could not come suddenly to her any more than it does to a nation. But the gifts we gave each other—the permission I extended to cry out, think aloud, and her willingness to endure my largely silent presence ("you choose")—these gifts are useful for little else. There were deeply troubling questions. Is independence wise? How useful are these gifts to achieve it? How can I know when I have it? Tensions were everywhere, between the ambition of the goal and the poverty of the means, between what had been an apparent success and what was only a wish for the future, between doctor and patient. Could she make it, and would I help? It might literally be the chance of a lifetime, perhaps the one chance, but more certainly it would reflect the chanciness of lifetimes. Was she too old to start again? How long could she endure being alone. Did she have the talent to create her own life? I was extending credit, but was I leading her not away from bankruptcy but toward an even greater danger?

The fact is, I never believed her complaints. Or, more accurately, I read them as signaling discontent, her present bankruptcy. She spoke with multiple voices and therefore could not be taken word for word. Paradoxically, I did believe in her, her capacity for liberation, her right to complain, the strength of her drive into life. I was at once profoundly disrespectful and respectful. By what warrant did I not take her at her word?

To me this is the most difficult question facing students of the psyche. Often I have sat with suicidal people and tried to decide how seriously to take the gesture—will my attention relieve or escalate the risk? I know of cases where the solicitude of the helper has challenged the endangered person to greater and greater tests of solicitude, even to the point of death. Do you care enough to save me even from that, particularly from that? There are also people at war with the world, who throw their full weight against every effort to help, until it breaks. Tested beyond strength, the helping person grows tired and withdraws; then the suicidal person's fury is released against the self. In these instances, too much solicitude can be lethal. But how to know whether the threat of suicide is a test or speaks for itself?

I said I heard a real voice in the patient. I didn't know this in the way you graph the action of the heart. There was something spontaneous, raw, unrehearsed, while her talk of suicide seemed a testing, almost measured, a show. Maybe someday we will measure the psyche as we measure the heart, but for now we work as old heart doctors did: feeling the pulse, tapping the chest, taking soundings.

Psychology, we hear, is the effort to be objective about the subjective. Physics often seems the effort to bring ever new subjectivities to bear on the objective, ever new and peculiar points of view, such as the extraordinary vision of Einstein. In everyday life I too act like a physicist, multiplying my points of view by seeking advice. I may also seek advice on my own subjectivity, the way I conceive things. It is often the goal of psychotherapy to reach after patterns of conceiving through the study of personal history and the developing therapeutic relationship itself: my subjectivity leaves its imprint on everything I do. Psychotherapy challenges the other's subjectivity by repeated exposure to the gaze of the therapist. Your way of looking at me meets my way of looking at you: the two subjectivities meet. The most complacent of us find it hard to ignore this persistent gaze. How does she see it? Even against the most stolid intention we may incorporate that gaze, the way we retain our parents' and teachers' ways of seeing. In such fashion we multiply our perspectives, in the direction of objectivity.

The incorporation of fresh points of view does not assure objectivity because one of these subjectivities may overrun all the others—you may see things only in the way your mother does. This is also the danger of psychotherapy. Probably psychotherapy's greatest contribution to objectivity is only the viewpoint that there are other viewpoints. I cannot trust myself, or you. I need many voices.

My patient saw things two ways. She was not at first aware of this because there was still no person separate from the two perspectives to reflect on the whole being. Consciousness was passed back and forth between two masters. One seemed to speak from the left side, the other from the right. Part of her would face around a little to listen to the other side in any sharp dispute. Many other times the two voices were mingled or one clearly uppermost, so that the level of inner separation was unclear. I discovered that often she wasn't talking to me as much as making announcements directed against the other part of herself. This was one reason she spoke so stridently or threatened so direfully, to be heard above her partner.

My patient's voices produced confusion, but also a richness of person that promised well for the future. Not much of the whole person was suppressed. Until I came on the scene, however, there was no one to listen to these rich subjectivities. The alternation of consciousness resembled a docile person forever voicing the last opinion provided. Also the voices echoed positions typical of her parents: the father earnest and conventional, the mother strident, disagreeable, almost without opinions unless they were contrary. It was easy to imagine why she had embraced the first. It was also easy to imagine why no voice of her own had emerged: they were both strong and intrusive. Perhaps she was lucky. If they had found common ground, she might never have heard her own voice. As it was, at least she had the independence of those small countries that play the superpowers against one another.

I listened to her voices. She watched my listening. I put it that way because she never asked what I thought. That would have meant assuming, if only for a moment, a viewpoint different from those she had. I think it was natural for her to accept my silence because part of her listened in silence to the contending voices. She had no discernible opinion about what went on. Did I?

I wanted to hear her out, to go on listening until everything was out. This meant encouraging the rebellious side, which was at first cowed. I couldn't listen for every word or nuance. That would have been exhausting and distracting, giving undue reward to much that was simply quarrelsome. Listening, I thought, meant as much waiting for the enormous quarrel to end. In the meantime astonishing things happened, often quite suddenly. She decided that she didn't like any of her friends, that everything passing between them was fake. She also quit her very successful job. The family was appalled. I was telephoned and threatened. I made no comment. They probably decided we were both mad. The patient defended neither me nor herself. To a remarkable extent we were each on our own.

Again, though, what was "my" own? For some reason I felt cheerful and encouraged. I was now and then shaken by her threats and pronouncements; yet even the gloomiest statement seemed to contain more of life than of death, and I hoped she would speak up. Sometimes she lay on the couch, almost tearing it apart. Most of the time she sat opposite me or walked around, singing bits of the songs she had begun to write. I laughed when I felt like it and occasionally looked grave. I answered questions but seldom said anything.

This was a strange sort of treatment. I felt grateful that Freud had the courage to start the tradition of silence and listening, the evenly suspended attention. That was not enough to explain my cheerfulness, however. There was her smile. In the midst of the most calamitous predictions she would break out into a smile: she looked healthy, real, alive. I couldn't imagine that anything was deeply wrong. But maybe she was in love with me or I with her, and our little *folie à deux* was just the usual enchantment dressed up as help. Perhaps, as was once suggested, psychoanalysis is the disease for which itself is the treatment. I want to reply that it is a cure for self-deception, which can be as lethal as cancer. But how is self-deception lessened by protests and silence?

I believed her protests and my silence were signs of a process through which her wishes and perceptions would appear and be acknowledged, even owned. Self-deception meant unacknowledgment or disowning. The battle between her two voices was a battle about ownership. This was the reason for my silence and the long, apparently aimless course of the treatment. I couldn't say, "Decide what's best for you," because there was no single "you" strong enough to respond. I had to listen for it, give permission for it to appear, above all let it work itself into existence against me and my silence. It had to grow, in a medium neither too critical nor too soothing. I couldn't say what was so tempting to say, "Make up your mind." She had been already too made up.

She had a way of walking into my office that made me think of a parade or a fashion show. Like a good soldier or a good model, she had an eye on the crowd; I felt like the crowd, so practiced and determined was she. Her entrance was not replaced by naturalness or ease; the parade turned into a rout or a charge. Now the rebel force was thrown not against her other side, but against me. Only the parents of happily growing children or therapists of the conventional know the full force of this rebellion—the ingenuity of abuse, the relentless scrutiny of error, the crowing contempt. The language of angry legislatures resembles it, or the scream of tabloids, but these are large, diffuse stages. In a small room, the emerging voice tests the fortitude of a Lincoln.

For a long time I was her image of convention, her gaoler, her Polonius. What could compensate for the loss of an enemy like that? Time streams through us on its way to the past, but so subtle is the passage that we think we remain the same; the residues of time recolor our organs of perception and we feel unchanged. Her anger was not so much discharged as slowly turned into a new view of life. She came to see convention, habit, and memory for what they are and, being able to do that, saw that I rejoiced in her clarity and force. The quiet walls and comfortable furniture were only a mocking surface, just as her successful life had been. We who had opened a sputtering dialogue between the present and the future could see that surface for what it was, a surface.

She had been the busy guardian of a tradition handed down by two frightened parents, competitive and struggling in every way they could find to adapt to an apparently alien culture. Now she found reasons to deplore that tradition far and near, its hypocrisy, the shallow personal relations it decreed, its apparent dismissal of any eccentricity or unconventionality that bespoke something novel or emerging, most of all the sense she had of nothing happening, of being frozen in time while the glimmerings of a different life tugged at her. Still she turned back to it as if there were nothing else palpable enough to point her way. The new life was only a protest, rents in a fabric that covered everything.

She had to stick her anger through that fabric over and over again until it hung disheveled and torn. Even then the sense of a real alternative came to her unpredictably as she chanced on elements in her daily experience that filled out the glimmerings. The most remarkable was a child, barely a year old, son of a neighbor, who responded to her with a directness and simplicity belying what she had learned. Children are often the refuge of those in search of the real, but this child was exceptional in his sturdy independence, open joy, unhesitating rejection of whatever seemed false. It was as if she had found the person she might have started to be, so she could both love him like the self of her own she was coming to love and stand apart from him as a miracle to follow. It is not enough to say that she looked forward to their visits and treasured them afterward; they were a key to what she wanted in all her life.

It was not a revolutionary program. The wisest ones do not want to expose their solitary heroic egos to a world at best indifferent. We all need to be respected and we wouldn't mind being rich. Most of the apparently heroic figures I have known are safe enough to defy the world, from positions long and well protected. So I helped her to know the world she deplored even as she sought some independence within it—to make sure that what she wanted for herself was not destroyed in its achievement.

Her ideal was to make music. Where once that had been what her conventional and respectable life pushed not only beyond her reach but beyond the right to reach, now it welled up in her as real, hers. Music, which had seemed insuperably beyond, appeared almost at the next moment within her. There is an old joke that relieves the solemnity of these proceedings. It is a necessary joke too, lest congratulation inflate the proceedings right back to surface and mockery. An opposing lawyer accused Lincoln of being two-faced. He replied, pointing at himself, "If I had two faces, would I wear this one?" The patient had put on another face. It was quite an ordinary thing to do. Once the proper primping she had done, all the attention to hair and clothes, preoccupied her; she had to be beautiful and pleasing. Her new freedom was also painful and arduous; she would find it useful to primp again, now and then.

I remark how ordinary the outcome was because I don't want to imply that we must all be artists or, least likely of all, great artists. There is a strong tendency to worship art, as there is to worship God. Whatever the merits of art and religion, they do not lie in worshipping, if only because it has usually meant worshipping priests and artists or, worst of all, some particular one. Her enthusiasm for success and appearances had been a flag waved against the darkness of the night. Any enthusiasm she now felt for her music was quickly sobered by teachers and critics. She discovered what serious workers always seem to discover, that any response to creation, even the greatest celebration, quickly loses its excitement: the reward is in the process itself, which is strangely impersonal.

She learned, for example, that one must welcome discouragement and anxiety in any creative task because they may be signs that will and control are giving way to something fresh and original. She had grown up among people who were convinced that anxiety was a sickness and not the freight of worry, even despair, that any difficult work carries with it. Now she saw anxiety as a warning of a change of feeling or point of view, of details that could signal new directions of work. She was being exposed to a singular existence of her own.

In time this process extended to her personal life. She had to wait for her friends as she did for her musical creativity. Early in life the great mixing bowls of school and college found her many like-minded people. Later the speed of mixing slows; the waits are longer. She was sustained by the change in her point of view. Being alone had once been an assault on her respect ability; respectability was no longer the foremost issue. She had come to want freedom of exchange. Friends were valued for their unexpectedness, the ways in which her former passivity was agitated and cleared. One gave her courage, another the curious experience of personal difference—one person held close and open to the gaze of the other. The uniqueness of these experiences made her all the more vulnerable to dread. When her friends had been numerous and almost interchangeable, the thought of loss hardly arose; now the solitary and precious were filled with the possibility of loss. She was discovering what Samuel Beckett called "the poisonous ingenuity of time in the science of affliction." The dearer the event, the more we can dread its end. The beloved child goes into a world that parents color with the horror of the child's being no more. We want to possess a loved one, yet the loved one is a spirit capable of being anywhere and with anyone, drifting away from us like smoke.

Love called on the same process that her music did. I remember her image of a colleague she loved, bounding, mercurial, both older and more naive than herself, loving her, wishing dimly for an affair, but groping and easily discouraged as he limped back home. His music was like that too, fierce but more showy than real. She was emerging from a similar state herself, loud and unsure; she would leave both this state and the man behind. Earlier there had been a stiff, lordly lover, full of bristling opinions; at that time she was still echoing her father's maxims. Remembering those images, almost mirror images of the men and her changing selves, I wait, as she waited, for the answering note in myself. Rainer Maria Rilke speculated in his letters on how Cézanne sought *realisation*. He would focus on the object. Then, "beginning with the darkest tones, he would cover their depth with a layer of color that led a little beyond them, and keep going, expanding outward from color to color, until gradually he reached another, contrasting pictorial element, where, beginning at a new center, he would proceed in a similar way." Inevitably there is a struggle between the objective element and the subjective answer waited for: her response to the men, mine to these images, Cézanne's paint creeping toward the real. It is the same in science. Knowledge is just hypothesis meeting experiment. So we wait. Someone would arrive to whom her subjective response was indeed a realization, a successful theory if you like, of the love she sought.

Yet nothing is over the way a play or a piece of music is over. In its passage time is colored by events and experienced as feelings. The separation of time and feeling is made by the clock and our responses, but this is only by way of understanding. Cézanne also separates his look at the motif from the paint his mind calls up, but the two come together as best they can in the realization, just as time and feelings make up a life. It is true that they gain weight in the form of memories, to the point of seeming to stand still. The future pushes toward us in anticipation of danger or more slowly in nervousness over what will befall, and it gains great weight and definiteness, like the past, in the expectation of a hated event. Love and home would mean new objectivities. What she would make of them, like Cézanne before his landscape, would depend on her capacity for life. Perhaps she would make something extraordinary of these ordinary elements, perhaps more remarkable than any song she wrote. Perhaps they would remain images or objectivities she could not respond to at all, leaving them like covers on a magazine.

Rilke also remarked about Cézanne that "no one before him ever demonstrated so clearly the extent to which painting is something that takes place among the colors." One has to leave them alone, to settle the matter among themselves. The work was very hard, impossible, but the painter could not afford to cogitate. It is an easy lesson to make absurd; somewhere he must be cogitating deeply. But I think Rilke meant that the answer cannot be forced or hurried; it has to spring up of its own, however controlled the conditions within which it occurs. We can say that successive conditions of freedom are created, little assemblies within which the state moves itself forward. The objective must be heard, and the subjective, and the whole mutinous crew held together. It is the same way with people in a family, which may require the greatest creativity of all, that opening out into the unbearable and unknown.

Otherwise we deceive ourselves dangerously. So we bend a little to the right or left, hoping to see and to hear.

10 ～ A Death

Many times we realize the existence of another only by aggravating the difficulties in a willful way—not responding or putting down wayward clues or setting aside everything obvious or intrusive—lest our minds be shaped by attractive images. Death and dying are often exceptions to that rule, as if life hurries forward to escape the death of the body.

The phone rang and a man, very likely dead soon of cancer, spoke. He was frank about his fate, taking his chances on whatever cure he might find, neither blind or self-pitying. This is part of what I mean by life coming forward. But was I ready to receive him?

Death is like great beauty, fame, or money in the self-consciousness it pulls from the observer. I had known this man a long time, before he was sick, and felt at home with him. He wanted to come now for help in saying goodbye to those he cared for. All his life he imparted great thoughtfulness, knowledge, and concern to everyone around him. He was always at the center of a problem, trying to solve it. Now the problem was his own death, but not its impact on him. He wanted to bear the pain of his going for others.

He didn't seem afraid of death. His fatigue was interrupting the tasks he liked, and he thought of many things he still wanted to do. Ye he wasn't as impatient with death as it seemed to be with him. They had a curious relationship. There was this awful thing growing inside him. Surgery, chemicals, and x-rays attacked it, but he stood to one side. Yes, he helped the surgeons, took the medicines, lay under the cold tubes. He even made important changes in the treatment. That didn't surprise me because I knew it was his habit to improve difficult matters. He was a remarkable contributor to my earlier efforts to help him. I felt it especially now. He didn't want me to suffer in his sickness. He was trying to make his parting easy for me too.

Nor did I want to burden him with my anxieties. He told me I made him feel better. At first I only knew he made me feel better about death. It didn't seem so formidable in his presence. I would have said he had risen above it if it were not so plainly all around him. This was the curious relationship between him and death—not in it together as friends, not as foes, more as acquaintances. I didn't see how death could understand this man, so full of life, if it understands anything. And I don't think he wanted to be close to death, although he was otherwise very curious. I could see him looking into death the way he had investigated many mysteries, quietly, unobtrusively. Perhaps the two were like those acquaintances one makes on an ocean liner. There can be a hint of romance or fatality, but the contact seldom feels permanent. God knows death makes many acquaintances and then passes on.

I think I pleased him because I was able to talk about his situation as we had talked about everything else. It took a while to get used to. There was the temptation to be sorrowful or stout-hearted or to hurry into a goodbye. What we needed to do was rest around the truth, the realization. But what was it, at least objectively? The doctors were not optimistic. One gave him six months, as if the doctor were Chronos with a prescription pad. He was in a very difficult spot, like a man surrounded by hungry cannibals, and would be lucky to get out alive. That was reason enough to do what he asked, to help him say goodbye to his family. At the same time, I didn't want to act as if it were all over.

This is a fine point, between a fatuous cheerfulness and the simply lugubrious. It is a generally useful point for most encounters with life, although I have never been steady there, pitching to one side or the other, like a dizzy captain. Being with the patient was therefore good practice for me. Perhaps it had some of the value of what Plato recommended, to practice dying. Again I feared the patient was more useful to me than I could ever be to him.

He was a good teacher. He could even tolerate a joke, which is the most exacting test of equilibrium in these circumstances, since a joke is generally about contrasts and he was at a place of sharpest contrast, between life and death. When my youngest child was three or four, she made her first joke, that there was an elephant in the refrigerator. Here again the joke is in the contrast. But that would not have been a joke for my patient, who was experiencing something worse than an elephant in a body increasingly cold and uncomfortable. The best I could do, as his hair fell out and his bowels tore at him like firecrackers, was to laugh at the wonderful hat he had bought and the jaunty angle he put it at. I thought of saying that the treatment was worse than the disease, but I knew he had chosen the treatment, with full knowledge, and the only thing worse than the disease was either death or not living up to his ideals.

There wasn't a great deal to say. We tried to sit and look them in the eye together, the horror and pain and uncertainty.

I cried more than he did, perhaps because he was braver and I was feeling sorrier for myself, that such a thing could happen. It's true that the living are the ones who suffer longer, especially when they have to live without the companionship of such a good man. I think he knew this, which was one reason for taking pains with his partings.

I suggested he tell the family members how much he loved them. I wanted him to be planted forever in their minds, and there are no better moments than extreme ones for that agriculture. I remember when my father was dying how openly he suffered, without drama or self-pity. When he felt pain he howled. That made it easier for me because I didn't have to imagine his pain or admire his nobility; it was all said and done. He made me see more clearly his great capacity to be free and natural without artifice or hypocrisy. It was as natural for him to howl as it had been for him to laugh or be angry. He loved an audience while never demanding or constraining it. I believe he not only planted himself in my mind for as long as I live but made this freedom a little easier for me.

Parting, especially parting for good, tests the completeness of our lives. Of course it tests the completeness of what we have given or what we might have given or taken. But the possibility of incompleteness on those scores is not so devastating as the incompleteness of being alive. This is what I have meant by the tyranny of image over the whole person suppressed. Dying becomes our last chance to experience one another. It is really as much a matter of saying hello as of saying goodbye.

There are endless distractions. I expect if I find a broken tooth or loose filling during my final hours, I will spend inordinate time tonguing it over. That's how far I am from the unhurried and untiring attention of mindfulness. My excuse would be that I don't want to think about dying. I didn't want to think of this man dying either. But I did want to experience him, not only because it might be my last chance but because I thought he deserved the same attention he had given to others, an attention he had not always received himself. I wanted him to experience my heeding him. The biggest distraction was death itself, which found ever new ways of intruding itself on the conversation, such as the way he looked. Saying goodbye is often destructive or perfunctory for just this reason. It can be our way of getting rid of something uncomfortable like death, rather than saying hello to something I wished would go on forever, his life. The distractions came up in a hundred ways. I found myself saying, "It's good to see you," when actually seeing him was like looking at a graveyard. In his forgiving way, he knew what I meant—that it was good to see *him*, the person I knew.

There was suspense in what we did. Could I pay attention? Would I put my foot in it? There was even high drama. Could his life emerge through so many signs of death? Was this the moment at which humans grasp the idea of resurrection, a rising from the dead, like out-of-body experiences? At no other time do mind and body seem so separate. Many fade out before their bodies do. He wasn't like that. New parts of him came to psychological life as he approached death. I don't want this to sound like a sentimental memory or a literary conceit. I want it to be obvious, the way the wall in front of me is obvious. To make it so we need a table of the elements of life similar to the table of chemical elements.

Once the elements of matter were believed to be fire, water, earth, and air. The chemists of the fifteenth century recognized sulphur, mercury, and salt. Today there are many more, but the list is provisional because it is empirical: others may be discovered and some may be broken down into still more fundamental parts. Let my search be seen in the light of this slow development.

I have already suggested that the soul is partly defined by feeling, feelings felt, the capacity for affective attunement. It grows by accretion, especially the accretion of conflict. Psychological life, for example, may be present in desire but even more when desire is mixed with awareness of the end of desire or the transcendence of desire. Another example is psychological-mindedness: the capacity to acknowledge other points of view, the acknowledgment of subjectivity itself. The soul, growing into conflict, has different points of view to own. Further, I suggested that people can be psychologically richer, like banks, by lending and receiving more. This unboundedness of psychological life, like physical extension, is evident when we enlarge ourselves by empathy or identification or by acts of imaginative extension, as in memory and fantasy.

The dying man showed me the elements of psychological life. He showed one in his very hesitation to return to treatment. He imagined how I might feel seeing him, looking his death in the eye. That imaginative act generated another, by the process of psychological reflection: he sensed I would not own up easily to my discomfort, and he needed to distract me for a while. These reflections were also projections, like the mirror's reflection; he had himself been discomfited by his appearance. But they were projections he acknowledged as part of humankind. He could believe a real disavowal as he could sense a false one.

The intensity of the situation, its extraordinary pain and danger, with all the possibilities of denial and outright flight, were also the impresarios of a real coming forth. I knew he had taken a chance on my concern for him. It was a brave bet. Perhaps he wanted to know, like the complacent lawyer, whether I bled. My imaginings of his motives were themselves a challenge. Perhaps he knew that too. But he gave me every chance a free person wants to be given, to retreat (he was never one to impose himself), to complain, to honor him.

The coming forth, then, was most dramatic because it had to pass through the strongest signs of death. He had become very thin; his thinness was everywhere, in his face, now like an uneven knife blade, his fingers, his legs without calves, a neck that barely seemed thick enough to hold up his head. His voice was thin too, often wavering. Yet, as you listened to him, the idea of his thinness fell to one side; his spirit noted it, even now and then called attention to it without regret or surprise, while the spirit itself, this psychological being, discussed his treatment, the doctors' uncertainty, the irony of being a guinea pig in a largely novel experiment, so rare was his tumor and so radical the attacks on it. The irony was that he himself had been a great student of medical experiments, had designed many, commented on more, and was now pioneering again, rather forlornly, he remarked. Today most people give their lives and bodies up to medicine, sooner or later, but his had been an almost lifelong gift, and here he was at the end, still hard at it. He was dying, as they say, with his boots on.

More often, in my experience, the thickness is in the body, the thinness in the spirit. The successful businessman was like that, mostly heft and connections. Sometimes it seems the rule, if only because most are wise enough not to wear their hearts on their sleeves. Perhaps the dying man could come forth so fully because it was too late for predation. It reminded me of Gandhi's advice, to be so poor, like an Indian village, that no one wants to bomb you. I don't think so. He had always been generous with himself. More likely it was the other way around: his infirmity gave him license to talk more about himself and how he felt; it may have put him a little less in the service of others.

It certainly put me in his service. I don't remember anyone I wanted to do more for. Partly this was because of his extraordinary attunement. He had always been among the least hysterical of people, if we mean by hysterical anyone dramatic and manipulative, anyone in whom honesty of feeling is a question. He had a rare simplicity. I would be tempted to say that most of the conventional images he might have used were beyond his strength and appearance, if I had not seen other dying people hold on to their pretensions to the end. Robert Louis Stevenson wrote, "To know what you prefer, instead of humbly saying Amen to what the world tells you you ought to prefer, is to have kept your soul alive." How does one stay in tune with what one prefers in this man's circumstances? Preference would appear a choice of pains or the hope for a moment free of pain or that forlorn cry, "How long, O Lord, how long?" It was death and the destruction of his body, not any glamorous image, that threatened to suppress the whole person. Yet he did not seem shaken by the image of death, any more than he had been impressed by other conventions in happier times. And the destruction of his body, with all those implications of ugliness and ruin, only excited his ingenuity and curiosity. It turned out that his body was remarkably like the rest of the world for him, something to use and explore. There was little proprietary pride. He seemed to rent it, so to speak, and was ready to move out when conditions became intolerable. They certainly threatened to become so, but in the meantime he went busily about, pumping out the cellar and repairing leaks in the roof.

He was obviously a hard man to suppress. He did not need much in the way of compensation for the images that sustain the rest of us. In the gentlest way he would tease me about psychiatric images, the wonderful conceptions that so often sustain our interest in patients. He would say that perhaps he was narcissistic for fussing over his colostomy. Happily I didn't say that, but it was a nice point. Since the students of psyche have great difficulty separating self-respect from self-adulation or self-care from overattention to the self, they are an easy target for anyone, like himself, who preferred Skinner to Freud. He believed, like Skinner and Sullivan too, that the world shapes people as much as people shape themselves, so we had better get busy reshaping the world. He kept at it, including this matter of my education.

When I suggested that he tell his family how much he loved them, I also said that he should tell them why—the memories of them he delighted in. Fortunately the ingenuity of time extends beyond affliction into some of the dearest things we have. Physical pain is difficult to remember, while we recover happy times with striking freshness. He recalled one winter afternoon he had spent with his daughter in the snow, the two of them sledding and shouting and spilling into happy drifts, out of which the little girl would bounce, laughing and loving. He met then the depths of her good nature, an affectionateness given with the same free hand he held out to others. He was not sentimental; he didn't cry, as I felt like doing, imagining those two kindred spirits, as close as humans get in this solitary life. I urged him to remind her of the day, so that it could reenter her existence. In fact she had forgotten the day; she wasn't sure she recalled it even after his description. It became like certain photographs of a childhood scene, when we never know whether we actually remember the event or recall only the photograph itself. But this was much more than a photograph. The memory was something she now had from him, like a new gift, although one she could not hold in her hand or show another person. It had an entirely psychological existence, illuminating her from within. She had only to think about it, if she was unhappy, to feel better. It came to stand for their relationship, uniting present with past, her childhood and adulthood, his fatherhood and old age; it was like a treaty of everlasting amity, a permanent credit. In the same, smaller way, people who have met a much-revered person can be fortified for years by recalling that person's smile.

They were a reticent family, so I also wanted him to tell his daughter, "And I know you love me too." She was afraid to tell him she loved him, I suspected, because it might sound final, and neither was ready to say goodbye. His saying "I love you" without a response from her left him hanging in the air, though it was good to remain quiet a while to let his declaration sound. He didn't have to hear her love; he knew it. She was the one who needed him to hear it. He wanted to leave them everything he could, to make his leaving a giving. The openness of her psychological being to him also opened him to her. Again, it was the volume of giving and receiving that measured the extent of their resources.

Neither would have said so, but they were attuning their feelings to each other. By speaking of what one felt for the other, they brought their feelings together, as people do who are newly in love. People in love delight each other this way, surprising and reassuring. What was secret and private, wishes and fears, open out into bright sunlight. My two were not newly in love; they were near the end. Yet in remembering and telling what they felt, they did something just as moving. Neither felt the same as the other; the memories and meanings were different. Moving them together, mingling the memories of love, made them possessions on the commons of their psychological existences: "I have your love." At the same time, the feelings were attuned, through finding words each could understand and smoothing out the dissonances that honesty must at first create. I don't mean that great music was written, masterpieces of love. But the feelings they experienced, the delight each felt, the sense of a great opening and mingling and closure too, was as if they were hearing music for the first time.

They discovered something else that those in love discover. The mingling of souls sets the imagination free. With those in love, it is the imagination of a future together. With the dying man and his daughter, it could not be that. Nor did they set to work imagining heavens on earth or above. What they began to imagine was parting, each from the other. I have said that life pushes forward all the more fiercely in the face of death. Now life and death looked each other in the eye.

There had been months when sickness was the whole theme, with death only a fear. This realistic man knew he might be dying, but he thrust that aside in his busy and effective management of sickness. Now his spirit began to flag; he sensed he was losing; death had its hand on his soul in the concrete sense of being a growing part of his psychological existence.

It was in keeping with his disrespect for mere respectability that, when death began to get the best of him, he made no protest about going. He never bewailed his fate, as the expression goes. He was not one to linger when his body had become so inhospitable. Still there was work to do. Again it was remarkable how he set about doing it: not dutifully but with a real sense of the benefits.

There was the matter of parting. How do you say goodbye? I remembered the most painful parting of my clinical life. The patient had come to me in a pretty pickle, and I had not been able to rescue him. He continued to come anyway, for whatever assistance he could get with the resulting disgrace and likely poverty. A series of legal maneuvers seemed only to postpone the inevitable. He spoke of killing himself if the last one failed. I knew there was no use hospitalizing him: he wasn't mad or even clinically depressed; he would soon talk his way out of the hospital and be still further disgraced. I hoped he would run far away, to start again. But he had no heart for that; he loved the life he was losing, which he had spent many painful years building.

I kept telephoning him, hoping we could meet if only once more. Each of these "once mores" was a parting. They gathered their pain from many places, from the affection I had come to feel for this gallant and forlorn man, from the hypocrisy I felt in myself—if I cared so much about him, why didn't I lend him the money he needed?—from the loss of a gifted person whose efforts had always been flawed. Moral ambiguities stuck to him like burrs. He had never had the confidence and sense of safety to do things right; finally the whole gèrry-built structure of his life collapsed. I could feel in myself the sickly ease of thinking he deserved it all, even after he had paid amply for his mistakes. I know how unforgiving society is for the kind of mistakes he had made. So I wanted to stick by him, not be part of the eager mob casting him out. He kept tempting me: "Oh come on, Les, can anyone care? Would I care for me?"

The dying man generated few moral ambiguities. He was easy to celebrate. But how to celebrate a goodbye without a certain hypocrisy, exceeding even the ruined man's goodbye? I thought of saying, I should be leaving, not you. Yet neither one of us could really believe that, however true. I had the lucky break and should at least not disdain enjoying it. Closer to the real was: I'm glad it's you and not me—which struck a chilling note. But I didn't feel as separate from him as that implied. What I felt was: you are going, I'm staying; it's rotten luck; I hope I prove half the person you are; I love you; goodbye.

The hardest part is sometimes the "I love you." Did I really love him? Would I want to live with him if he lived at all? And how dare say those words when physicians are being wisely defrocked for seducing patients or allowing themselves to be seduced? Yet there was a real sense in which I had come to love him, as is the case often with patients we accompany a long way. I didn't want to sleep with him or live with him. But I felt something I wanted him to know, in this time of facing death.

Once I told another patient I loved him, a sad man who didn't believe he could be loved. He was gay, and I knew I might be misunderstood. I thought we could survive that mis-understanding and come out the other side stronger for it. Eventually he told me he was afraid he had seduced me, that I might leave my wife and children, and he didn't want that. He had gained the strength to ask me if it was true. I told him no—

I just loved him. He was relieved. He also said he thought the great changes in his life sprang at least in part from what I had said and from the courage he felt I had shown in saying it. It is true that I had been afraid.

To the dying man I couldn't say what we say to so many: just survive your miseries; they'll serve you well. That is the old story of the death of an egotism he never had. His miseries would indeed be the death of him—but not before there was another coming to life. If he had a fault, it was his obedience to those he pitied. This sometimes waylaid his naturalness, pulling him out of shape to bear what others should have borne alone. For the time left he seemed largely free of that, whether from fatigue or from a real freeing up. He just waited, and the self-pitying ones found their own way. For my part I looked on with relief.

His level-headedness before disease persisted in the face of death. I thought this his greatest claim to psychological life. Philosophers say that the idea of being needs the idea of nonbeing; there is no having one without the other. He kept faith with his mortality, we can say; he didn't desert it for a pious heaven. In the same way he kept faith with his uncertainty and curiosity, and in clinging fast to his ideals, at once so modest and so grand, he didn't sell out. To let the unknown be unknown—what a measure of vitality, when the unknown is death! Such has often seemed the supreme test of soul, this capacity to remain faithful when every pull is toward superstition and salvation. He went on looking death straight in the eye.

His time came, and not while he was with me. I am glad he will not suffer more and not have to worry about me. We do not pay our way. What this man gave was like a great scholarship to the university of life. He was too modest to speak of wanting to be remembered, but I want him to be remembered, to hear what only the survivors hear, because in his case the high-flown words are true.

11 — A Birth

The directness he carried into the room stood out only for a moment, when confusion, a real bewilderment, took its place. I was to feel both states one after the other, many times, until they merged toward the end into something skeptical but steadfast.

Vaguely dissatisfied with what many called a successful and happy life, he had gone back to school at thirty-five and was suddenly surprised. The teacher had put the class to writing their lives. He told me there were long periods before his twenties when he could remember almost nothing. Now he felt like a stranger to himself, this man so popular, steady, seemingly robust. What he did remember were flickering images, the corner of a room, someone's face, a hillside. And he felt afraid of what he couldn't remember: a darkness behind, out of which must come the very old and terrible.

He fled that class, though the teacher had been kind and unsurprised. His fear continued; he went back and asked the teacher what to do. Was it like those stories so often told, when people wake up in distant cities unmindful of how they got there and with no remembered pasts? Sometimes they return, and sometimes their pasts return. Often they are accused of wanting to escape a difficult present. It is never easy to know how much is real forgetting and how much a useful story.

My patient didn't appear to be escaping anything in the present. He did feel he was escaping, and only barely escaping, something dreadful in the past. His mother and father were dead. He began to question his two brothers and sister. They said what had always been said: he was a successful student, well liked, a natural leader, a solid pillar of school and community. He himself remembered honors he had received, and some teachers. Yet he could see or feel little else.

The man was a computer engineer. He told me he felt programmed. When I asked him who had done the programming, he said he didn't know, then thought of his older brother. This brother had recently humiliated him, in a puzzling way. The brother accused him of stealing two books. The patient was a great reader, so he assumed he must have borrowed the books. At the same time, he couldn't recall either borrowing or taking any books from the brother's house. Had he forgotten this too?

He discussed the accusation with his sister. She was a timid woman and loath to talk about it; she was famous in the family for doing whatever the older brother asked. Under pressure from the patient she blurted out, "You've been stealing for years."

A second brother was closer to the patient and less under the older brother's thumb. He said he had heard these accusations before and never knew what to say. Once the older brother had also accused him of stealing, which he denied. But he was reluctant to confront the brother.

I could feel the ground slipping away from the patient: his past, self-esteem, family relations, much of what gave meaning to his life. He said he thought he might go mad. He had lost some of the connections that secure a mind, making it familiar to itself, in fact more coherent than it freely is; he lost a measure of that usual stability provided by knowledge of where we emotionally are, who is with us, what they will do. He didn't lose his mind, which most often occurs under the pressure of intolerable fear or rage when the mind literally explodes, scattering away from an emptied core. Nor did I think he would lose it, because of his clear perceptions, his convincing reports to me, all indicative of a functioning center. But his surprise, the extent to which appearances had deceived him, suggested a weak self-awareness. Here might be an important place for coming to life.

I liked him. His bewilderment made me feel useful, and his simplicity and directness were appealing. More than any of these natural sources of affection was the pleasure I felt in a task to be joined, something we could do together, in this great business of making a life. So we set to work. Or rather I set to work, since he was confused. It is the sense of an unexpected goal that sets the stagnating world in vital motion; cast that aside, or make it only a intellectual exercise, and everything moving and growing is lost.

I said I was lucky to have him here, that it was a privilege to be with him, his mystery mine to solve. What should he do, he asked? Nothing, nothing, I said—that's my job. He had enough on his hands already, the bewilderment, accusations, the powerful brother, the darkness behind. All that would keep him busy just to stay on his feet. A demoralized person needs most the perception of an active, responsible helper. We could not yet investigate or plan; he could hardly exist until he felt the crisis pass. The obvious satisfaction I took in him and in the possibilities of his life declared that I was not dismayed or hopeless. The work could begin.

It began ominously. He phoned the brother, denied the charge, and was called insane. The brother said he had disgraced the family and would be welcomed back only if he made a full confession. He announced, "I will pray for you." The patient was staggered, but he was able to describe this brother as someone he had never understood or fully trusted, a rigid, pompous boy and man, a leader of his church, impossible to contradict. True, the brother had protected the younger children against the father's rages and arranged the mother's hospitalizations when she was depressed; and the family still circled around him, spent holidays in his home, went to him for help. Yet there was a regular practice at the end of every holiday dinner that the patient recalled with disgust: each younger person sat on his lap or at his feet, when he would hold the person's head, say a prayer and whisper advice, then give a blessing. The patient said he was the only one who refused to do this.

He remembered other details. They didn't emerge clearly or from an orderly perspective. They burst in, like little explosions through a narrow crack of light. I let them shape a story in my own mind.

He remembered overhearing the brother tell his sister about a speech the patient had given in school. It was not the same speech the patient remembered giving, but flowery, soaring, delivered to wild applause, and full of the brother's favorite ideas. Actually the audience was a small class, largely bored. The same happened again, after a track meet, this time with the patient's other brother. Later the older brother's tone changed, after the patient first declined the dinner ritual. The patient remembered turning to see the brother staring at him with black, furious eyes; his voice was even calmer, more soothing and commanding than usual. The patient recalled shivering, as if in the cold.

Once his sister was describing a Christmas years before when the mother was alive. She began quite spontaneously to tell how slowly the mother unwrapped her presents, how she stopped at one point while everyone waited, staring blankly at the presents. The brother interrupted quickly, "It was not like that," and turned the conversation away.

Then, breaking in as if for the first time, something between a memory and a dream gripped the patient. He was walking alone in the woods behind their house, heard the crack of a stick and turned to see, in the falling twilight, the older brother pulling up his pants. He thought he saw his sister running away in the distance. Later he questioned her (she was about twelve); she blushed and ran to her room.

What grew around the patient now was an unfamiliar loneliness. He had felt part of the family, clean and proud despite his misgivings. Now the family receded and darkened. Only the younger brother and a niece kept in touch, and he was afraid to question either one. He was also afraid to question me, he said, because of what I might tell him, that they were all corrupt or mad or unforgivable.

He found himself crying suddenly, becoming enraged, or so preoccupied that it was like awaking from a dream. Once a fellow worker asked him if he was all right after the patient had broken off their conversation to stare out a window. More and more he asked himself the same question. Why was he preoccupied with himself, selfishly he said, when all his life he had seldom thought like this? He wondered out loud if he had ever been aware of himself. He recalled puzzlement at classmates in high school telling of their self-consciousness. He never understood what they meant.

Another blow came from an unexpected place. Almost without knowing it, he had been feeling bit by bit more isolated from his wife. Theirs had been a perfect marriage, he said. They never quarreled, they enjoyed the same things, and every problem fell away easily. He found himself thinking: she reminds me of someone, someone I know very well. He had a curious new feeling of being with her and yet not with her at all. When I asked him to associate to this feeling, he said nothing. Then: "You won't believe this. I don't believe it. You know, she's just like my oldest brother. If she wasn't a woman, half his age, almost half his size, I'd say she was him. Oh, my god!" I thought oh-my-god too. I know many people who seem to have married their most difficult family members, and it was never good news. Did this man have to start over, with both his families?

I believe we shrank away from each other for a moment, he perhaps sensing my fear, I wondering if such a start was possible. He had already caught my imagination; now, I thought, he was testing my loyalty. It would be far easier to desert him now than later; I should leave at once if I was to leave at all. Perhaps there is a moment like this in the history of all efforts to be of help, when the water suddenly deepens and you realize you might drown. Just by remaining you commit yourself, and I could not leave.

I suppose these half-conscious processes, settling a long course of action with hardly a word spoken, carried as well some upward movement of my heart, some hardening around a point of work. I could not have explained my next words, nor did I want to. It was one of those moments in which you collect yourself, assert a self-possession when not long before your resolutions were scattered about, unpacked, unmoving. "A pretty pickle," I said seriously. He smiled, as much to himself as to me—there could be no forgetting or denying now. I felt his spirits rise, perhaps because this was no longer a challenge he faced alone but also gallantly, as if there were nothing else he could do.

It was quite another matter to decide what to do. Alone in both his homes, steady only in his work, a stranger also to himself, any new getting acquainted, whether in making a new home, changing the ones he had, or coming to terms with himself, now centered on me because I had been in at the beginning of this sudden birth of consciousness. It made me like a parent, a useful fact for this parentless and now perhaps familyless man. No doubt he would bring his real parents into the relationship with me, but that would not be pure distortion since I was in fact like a parent, both in helping give birth and in having some responsibility for the outcome. This is part of what I mean by the water deepening.

These somewhat pompous reflections fled my mind entirely when he looked hard at me and said, "What are we going to do?" I tried not to look bewildered myself, although I probably didn't succeed. I had to tell the truth: "I don't know." That bluntness may gave given me the courage to add, "We'll think of something."

I write these words in a similar spirit. To catch in retrospect what I hazard was being born between us and in his life, to describe the sparks of difference and opportunity I tried to fan into a flame, to do this without the most manifest distortion—I feel as I felt then, perhaps it is beyond me, but perhaps "I'll think of something." We wait for the squalls to pass, for some moment of calm that allows the mind its natural operation, its power to toss up possibilities, even solutions, if only we let it work. This is easier as I write than it was in front of a desperate man who was all but hollowed out by an extended history of pretense and was without his usual fronts and hopes. But, happily, most catastrophic awareness penetrates slowly and partially: like a defeated nation, the violated mind preserves outposts, broad stretches of untouched countryside that a detached observer would think still safe and flourishing. Besides, my relative calm served to rally those outposts and give the whole disorganized retreat an appearance of little victories here and there.

Of course, as the patient left my office with nothing resolved and a small, gerrymandered future shoved into place at the last minute, the week to come seemed to stretch like an eternity, for both of us.

He had in fact no one else to go to, but he didn't know that yet. His whole will flung itself against the older brother; every free thought directed itself to reaching and changing the brother's mind. Later, even when he wished consciously to avoid the brother, most of his mind still struggled in the same direction. At first he wanted to believe that his brother misunderstood him, would come around in good time. When it became clear that this would not happen, he wanted to persuade the brother, then make threats, and finally take revenge on this immobile man who seemed to embody the whole force of a lifelong compiracy to deprive the patient of all access to awareness. A conspiracy? Paranoia? I could have taken the patient for a madman—as he himself had at first—if I did not suspect that the chief madness lay in the brother's intransigent placidity, his blank refusal to acknowledge error, memory of events others recalled, or feelings of any kind. He stood as the image of perfection, demanding full obedience, ruthless in exiling any rebellious person or thought. The patient might well go mad if he threw himself with too open a heart against such intransigence.

This is the story of a birth in many ways. First of all, it was a birth of consciousness, or self-consciousness. But what is this self that comes to consciousness? A teacher asked him to give an account of himself; little came to mind. Then he confronted a self he did not recognize, the liar and thief his brother alleged. So who was he? He could present a name, a wife (there were no children), his profession, relatives, a hobby or two, a liking for olives and hot dogs. None of these sufficed. Moreover, he had a commonplace name he'd never liked, and a face like many others. Who was he?

Maybe he was a madman. That at least is an identity. Sadly it is an identity of exile, once into distant, rural asylums, now onto homeless city streets. Like most people, he dreaded such a fate. Yet it felt like what his brother wanted, as if the patient's name could be wiped from the pages of the family history, reduced, forgotten, put down as an aberration of brain and gene.

He chanced on me, who is not so clear himself as to what makes up consciousness and self. I didn't think him mad and also thought I saw the beginnings of a real person, in abilities, dreams, and strivings that might grow into consciousness. I didn't want such labels as thief or madman or paranoid to be in on those beginnings. They are great weights to carry through life, able to narrow or destroy the strongest spirits.

I thought, probably his brother wished he had died, preferably in one of those innumerable accidents that leave mankind relatively free of shame and responsibility and allow correct sentiments to accompany the disappearance of the victim. Then the brother would have no one to challenge him, no irritating dissident to his seamless family account with its decorous tones of harmony and love. And far better than a suicide which, though preferable to outright war, leaves behind black marks and unforgettable emotions.

Those would have been identities—madman, thief, early death, suicide—that claim many. What did I have to offer? The brother's passion for order and control established part of *his* identity. Was there any such passion to animate my patient? In the radical change that absorbed him, he had one advantage over others who are stripped of their illusions and must rebuild circumstances, purposes, an identity and history to sustain them. He was disillusioned but was not deceiving himself; he was innocent and did not feel ashamed. Further, the very passion of his brother's dominance excited responsive dominances of his own. First they were thrown against the brother; now they could be thrown into the construction of his life. These things he owed the brother: an example of what he didn't want to be and a dim realization of the force it takes to be anything of your own in this hard world.

I think too that his innocence and sudden disillusion joined to provide an opportunity much more difficult to exploit by those whose awareness is mixed with guilt and remorse, those whose nakedness must be hidden, most of all from themselves, out of shame. He faced life without pretense, he could be simply human, and he could survive; and the very monstrousness of the brother's pretenses rendered still more valuable his lack of them. Perhaps this was only his old innocence in a new form, but I didn't think so. It occurred with a growing self-consciousness. Moreover, it added an irony and humor that felt new.

My own part in this was largely admiring, of his stalwartness, directness, and readiness to look at his new situation with unclouded eyes. The misstep I most feared of myself was insincerity, any spoiling of the simplicity and directness that in his desperation he might abandon for a fresh pretense. Yet I didn't want to be distant, to seem neutral or aloof. I felt a kind of love for him, as you might for a newborn. I remembered one woman whose fragile presence in the world could not believe and hardly bear even mild statements of admiration. So I needed to repeat them over and over again. Several times she had dropped her cold mask of perfection before others, only to have her thin, eccentric presence swept away by the appalled onlookers. I wanted her to try again with me and, as part of any such willingness, she needed to know of my affection for her. I had talked about her spirit, her brave willingness to try again, the reality of her anguish, but none of that was quite right. Once I heard an advertisement on the radio for an expensive foreign beer. The dialogue was between an awkward young man and a smooth lady. He kept asking her if she served him the fancy beer because he was handsome or bright or promising. When each time she answered no, he insisted on knowing why she did it. She replied, "I thought it would help." I thought my speaking out would help too. The patient remarked, "It's just part of your business." I returned, "Yes, it is—a wonderful part, these realities that occur in therapy." She was a teacher who, I knew, loved many of her students, so I added, "It's part of your business too." This she could acknowledge, which brought the realities of my feelings closer to home. And like the woman in the ad, I didn't do what I did because of some wonderful quality in the patient, but for something else, something deeper, more general, a human note that had been struck between us. And of course it helps.

I had been trained not to say such things, to express affection, for many convincing reasons. Yet I came to feel that training is what you do to dogs or seals or soldiers, hardly the background for therapists. The teachings I received set an inhuman pall on the work, often thick enough to kill it. Certainly patients could, even should, speak of their love for us, but never the reverse. How can such matters be a one-way street? Worse, I came to suspect that the unspeakability of love—which is as commonplace among therapists as it is among teachers—might explain why it is so often acted out in abuse and seduction. We are all taught to talk, not act. Maybe there would be less acting out if there were more speaking out.

Now, the steadfast man didn't need so much speaking out as the fragile woman, but there were many times he needed my strong admiration to sustain him. It was easy to supply; it would have been as unnatural to withhold what I felt as it would for him to suppress his terror and loneliness. The real, I thought, waits for a voice to call to it, "Come out, be heard." Once more pretense and an artificial calm could be set aside, by both of us.

The long course of remembering and enduring that lay before us had one feature I never experienced so strongly before. He seemed to pass through the memories and crises with equilibrium, in sharp contrast to what I felt until a little before the end. I was on a rollercoaster ride. One week I would feel clear and in charge. At the next visit everything would unravel, my understanding, the context he had developed, even the possibility of change. Desperately I learned to sit tight and wait: this too will pass. I also learned the source of many of these upsets, the extraordinary brother. It was a case study in the social dynamics of paranoia.

I knew something of how insiders drive outsiders mad. Yet I had never seen the process so close and sharp. First the outsider is isolated, with a consensus created against him. At the same time, he is politely received, especially by the leader; there is nothing to complain about; the group feels normal and fair. At this the brother was a master. His coolness, quietness, utter evenness of tone exuded conventional sanity. He could deal with outbursts of feeling so calmly that the complainer appeared the perfect picture of madness and he of sense. And the evenness had the wonderful effect of driving the complainer to still greater bursts of feeling, so that the neutral onlooker was given a textbook instance of the mad versus the sane. All the brother had to do was to mention the patient with a sigh, with the briefest comment on his behavior, and the consensus was his. The lesson: you would have to be mad yourselves not to agree.

I suspect the patient's equilibrium was so little upset by these confrontations (in contrast to my own) in part because he couldn't believe they were happening. Even worse, at the start he agreed with the rest that he must be mad. With less support he might have gone off willingly to the asylum. He did become depressed as the difficulty of his situation reached him, but he had a remarkable, perhaps constitutional steadiness of outlook (like the older brother's) which served him well. For this reason our work vividly illustrates what I think is the central drama of psychotherapy: the collision and exchange of viewpoints. Before the collisions occur, people are like ships in the night: they may send occasional signals, show a light or two, travel together for a while, even come to believe they have the same destination. But in fact each sees the other through his or her own eyes; they are insulated, like different species. It is true that people conclude on the basis of bits of behavior or expressed ideas, but these are constructions in the observer's mind, far away from actual experience of the other. We also think we understand people because of similarities of appearance or shared emotions, most often perhaps on the basis of a common purpose, while even the most apparently intimate connections of this sort can emanate from points of view utterly remote from our own.

In Joseph Conrad's story "The Return," a successful young London merchant comes home to his beautiful ordered house, secure in his conviction of being a respectable member of the upper classes. He enters his dressing room, the closets hung with mirrors, and throughout the story he sees himself in the several images thrown back from the merciless glass. A piece of paper lies on the table, a note from his wife, saying she has left him. All at once the perfect image is shattered; he is shamed, angry. He struggles to understand, but foremost is indignation, stemming from his eminent, untouchable position. He seems to shout, "How dare you affect me?" Unexpectedly the wife returns; she can't carry through her wish to join the other man. Now he has the traitor before him. He is relieved but torn by curiosity about what she has planned and done, and fearful of dropping again from the lofty position in which such curiosity is ignoble. He wants to forget, even forgive, but incorrigible doubt has entered his mind and he must silence it. Desperately he tells her he loves her. She replies, "You are deceiving yourself. You never loved me. You wanted a wife—some woman—any woman that would think, speak and behave in a certain way—in a way you approved. You love yourself . . . If I had believed [you loved me] I would never have come back." He is dumbfounded. Her perspective has been opened to him; his is shaken. She implies: ours was a respectable arrangement, useful, safe, what I wanted, at least for a while, but there was no place for love in it. We catch a glimpse of why she left and why she returns—she had wanted love, lost heart, and settled for appearances. On the other hand, he thought he had love, and certainly loved appearances. The perception of her inner life acts like a mirror-light reflected back on his own. Love and faith, both terribly shaken, become his stated ideals, and he loses faith that he can find love in her. It is as if the glimpse of her failed love has ignited his own wish. She retreats from love back into appearances. He loses interest in appearances, at least for a moment, while groping blindly for love. He then leaves, never to return.

This is why I call the collision of viewpoints the central drama of therapy, perhaps of our lives together. Disillusioned with her artificial world and driven to expose that disillusionment, the wife exposes the merchant's world to her perspective. He can see her for a moment and, in seeing her, see something of himself. The fabric of their blind, successful life together is split open. The splitting could probably not have occurred if she had not also conveyed the poignance of her disillusionment; she is laid open. And the very relentlessness of his attack on her exposes more and more of her wreckage. She has not only lost the stability of appearances, but faith in her capacity to love, even to hide. He emerges the luckier one, though his capacity for love was untested.

My patient, like the defeated wife, had thrown himself against images of the imperial brother. Perhaps if the patient had come limping home, like the wife, and given his wreckage up to scorn, he too might have penetrated the brother's ramparts. But I didn't want the patient to end like that, to be an occasion for the brother's development. I wanted the patient to find the love he needed. This meant changing his view of the appearances his brother had created, having the experiences of both the merchant and the wife, being disillusioned and ignited, exposed but better protected. To that end I hoped he would see into my perspective and have that reflected back into his own.

I believe, however, that what makes possible such effective collisions is the limitations, if not the wreckage, they reveal. People don't change because they perceive a new truth or want to change. The experience of seeing into my perspective needed a force comparable to what the merchant saw, a force that pierces and changes views hitherto solid, seemingly invincible. The merchant needed the wife to maintain *his* viewpoint, in order to realize its bankruptcy.

This became possible when I took the brother's place as the parental figure to whom he turned. The brother wanted the patient to confirm an image of family correctness, but I introduced a revolutionary element: he was to see both the brother and me not from our viewpoints but from one of his own. This meant, when he looked at me for the truth, he saw me looking at him for it—and the force of that reversal had to repel a great beseeching. Already I had compromised my position, by thinking I understood the brother, so it was important to retreat from any such confidence lest I discourage him from exploring for himself. A still greater difficulty lay in his desperation, which called out for that very confidence, my knowing the truth.

I could receive his hope kindly, I could sympathize with the pain of not knowing, I could say how much I wished I knew, how I too yearned for truth—but what did he think, how did he see it? For a long time he played at this like a game, secretly half-believing I was only waiting to announce the truth. Unlike the merchant's wife, I didn't want to leave a note in the hall of mirrors to shatter the homecoming. I wanted no detonation at all, more a slow dawning, something like the discovery of a child that he is bigger and older and can move.

The memory of his brother in the woods had been like a lighted fuse sputtering in his mind. He could never be sure the incident happened. The other siblings met his accusations with a kind of unassenting belief that mirrored their own confusion. Perhaps the memory delayed any real emancipation because it set the patient in stark opposition to the brother, as empty of any perspective of his own as obedience had been. Such oppositions had always been the brother's forte: others were for him or against him. There was no place for skepticism, individuality, mixtures of sense and nonsense.

The emergence of an independent viewpoint in a mind owned or conventionalized is a tantalizing thing. We may think the independent viewpoint has arrived; then it disappears, only a familiar tyranny dressed up to please us. Opposing signs can emerge together: sometimes the patient would stiffen, utter a platitude, and in the next breath say something I never heard before. The experience of suddenly encountering a new person in the old clothes is both unmistakable and elusive. Am I imagining it? Will it return?

The process is very slow. But that's as it should be, because a rapid emergence is likely the putting on of a fresh mask. Something as broad and multifaceted as a new mind needs good time in which to grow, and it must be tested, reflected on, abandoned, then picked up again, as small acts of self-possession replace the old conformity. "I mean this," he would say, an expression from him new to me, perhaps a signature of his mind working its way across an event, the words suggesting he had somehow penetrated the event, identified connections. It is a large part of what it means to be human, this penetration to what may be either deep or shallow. Thus we say, only a human being could have said anything so foolish.

Just when I thought he had finally emerged, he would retreat again. It was as if he would not give me the satisfaction of being himself. Or perhaps it was the final liberation, to be free of me, a place he could not reach until I had given up caring what he was. How was I to do that? He is testing me again, I thought. He wants to know whether I really believe in his freedom or only wait to see him do what I want. He is like an actor, I thought, playing different roles, not to intrigue the audience but to drive it away. That would make sense: the play is over and we are all supposed to go home.

It was the end of my working day, at the end of winter, which where I live goes on and on, hints of spring come and gone, until at last we give up expecting and just let it happen. It seemed that way with my patient. Again I recalled what one of my teachers said: the idea is to bore the neurosis to death. Here it was the other way around. He was boring me, not to death but to his own life. I had to let go my expectations, as in a fit of ennui, while he went off on his own. So I said nothing, let my mind wander, the way we should when the patient is no longer any of our business. I knew if he needed me he would call me back or wake me up. Meantime I could muse on by myself, perhaps even look after my own self-possession, as befits someone who had been so long concerned with his. Is it always this way in the happiest of outcomes, I wondered, that the other person moves past us and makes it tactfully evident that we have to examine ourselves? I had often seen it with younger people during their strong growing times. The moment arrives when you know you are being left behind. Many did it so quietly, with such little fuss or sense of superiority, that I could return to my work undisturbed, perhaps starting on something new of my own.

The day had seemed long and this hour, one of our last times together, felt long too, as time stretches itself when nothing in particular happens. I had been off daydreaming when he remarked on the spaciousness of the room we had worked in—he hadn't noticed before. He also said he didn't know how to "terminate," the sad, dire term often used on these occasions. I thought to myself that we do terminate others sometimes, ourselves too; I have terminated some relationships I wanted no more of. But I didn't know what it would mean to terminate this relationship. I would like to have the memory of it forever, and I would like him to return to it if he ever needed to. In truth I wanted the relationship to last a long time, until one or the other of us was actually terminated, lasting like a bridge he could step on to return. I thought, the psychologically real announces itself in feelings that carry the idea, this may not mislead me, this has permanence, a recognizable place in one's enduring sense of things. I now had this feeling about the once-beleaguered man, a feeling I could not terminate if I wanted to. If we were to say goodbye, if he were going away to the ends of the earth, that would only deepen the relationship, which is what people experience in many goodbyes when they touch each other intensely for a moment, in the hope that a moment of heat will solder the relationship forever.

I didn't want to say these things. Augustine wrote that to love is to let be, and this man was going off after this search for his own perspective. In any case, how many of us have words for such occasions? I could wish him good luck, so central to all our dealings with the world. Certainly I would miss him. But one recovers quickly from such happy losses, is in fact better for them, as if the relationship is moved inside to cement our own selves more strongly together.

~Postscript

In this book I began with the image, drawn to it as we all are, then worked toward the person suppressed. Coming to life is a discovery, creation, development, a setting free and also a containing of that person. Behind this apparently simple structure lie many perspectives formed by theories and schools that shape and absorb one another over long periods, and through their struggles ensure a real continuity to the work.

The diverse and meandering paths to life have elements in common: the creation of a psychological space in which people can be met as much in their strengths as in their disabilities, as much to discover the future as to examine the past. The goal is detecting health and oppositions to health and the movements we can make to give power to the one and support against the other. Such a psychological space furthers seeing the drift of a life amid innumerable events and cultivating the attitudes we need to gain possession of that life, in particular the power to bear the full range of feelings that relationships demand, either with others or for work. Too many retreat before the best they might have.

Yet every account of what we do distorts the organic nature of all these interactions as well as the curious mixture of letting alone and occasional nudging which is the task. As time passes, that task seems to me more and more a matter of growing things, of movements and feelings, and less a matter of words and ideas—in which my own effort, too, may be imprisoned.